So This is Africa!

Betty Kilgour

Best Wishes

Betty Kilgour

Detselig Enterprises Limited
Calgary, Alberta

Betty Kilgour
Three Hills, Alberta

Canadian Cataloguing in Publication Data
So this is Africa!

ISBN 0-920490-73-5
1. Kilgour, Betty – Anecdotes.   2. Tanzania – Biography –
Anecdotes, facetiae, satire, etc.   3. Tanzania – Description and
travel – 1981 –   I. Title.
DT440.5.K44 1987   967.8   C87-091238-0

© 1987 by Detselig Enterprises Limited
P.O. Box G 399
Calgary, Alberta T3A 2G3

SAN 115-0324
Printed in Canada   ISBN 0-920490-73-5

This book is dedicated with love to our children:

To Beth, my little cohort in so many weird and wonderful happenings,

To Mitchell for listening to her stories,

To Margaret
Judy and Brian
Pat and Merle
Ian and Kelly

Thank you for your staunch support while we were in Tanzania and for allowing us to go in the first place! May your children give you the same opportunity to live a wonderful adventure.

Acknowledgements

There are many I wish to thank for their assistance and support:

Laurel Enright for her excellent editing and polishing,

Pete Cote for hours spent proofreading,

Leona Loosmore for having the foresight to save all the letters and reports we sent from Tanzania,

Ben Crane, my wonderful illustrator,

Ted Giles for taking another chance with my material,

Helge Lein for providing some of the pictures,

Chris Bryant, executive director of CUSO, for writing the foreword,

CUSO for giving us the opportunity to go in the first place,

And last but certainly not least, President Nyerere and the people of Tanzania, for according us such a welcome and such love while we were stationed in your marvelous country.

This book is not a documentary on Tanzania, nor is it a handbook on volunteering. It is not Bill's story – that is for him to tell. Rather, it is my adventures, along with a few of Beth's and Bill's, in a strange and wonderful land – some funny, some sad and lots interesting. The thoughts and beliefs I express are mine and mine alone; feel free to disagree. Just read with a light heart and enjoy!

Detselig Enterprises Ltd. appreciates the financial assistance for its 1987 publishing program from

Alberta Foundation for the Literary Arts
Canada Council
Department of Communications
Alberta Culture

Betty Kilgour, with her husband Bill, lives near Three Hills, Alberta. A writer of articles, short stories and poetry, she is well known for her weekly column which ran for ten years in newspapers throughout Alberta. In addition to her posting in Tanzania, she served two years as a volunteer on Niue Island in the south Pacific. She has five grown children.

Foreword

I don't know Betty Kilgour – or Bill or Beth – except from the pages of this book and some brief phone conversations. I don't know Tanzania either. You might well ask why I get to write an introduction to this book. Well, I do know CUSO, and I have worked with many people like Betty over the years in other countries where CUSO works.

For my sins I got to be Executive Director of CUSO and now spend most of my time far removed from the kind of field experiences Betty describes, but I do remember them well – and miss them.

Since 1961, CUSO has sent more than nine thousand people to work in over sixty different countries around the globe. Bill McWhinney and Dave Godfrey, in *Man Deserves Man*, told a few of the nine thousand stories. Ian Smillie in *The Land of Lost Content* told some of the history of CUSO and a few more of the nine thousand stories, but many, many remain to be told.

Betty, who has told some fine Canadian stories in *The Best of Crocus Coulee*, has put her Tanzanian experiences on paper in this book. Her story is clearly a unique one; her work, her experiences, her family cannot be exactly duplicated by any other CUSO worker. However, themes run through Betty's story that other CUSOs will recognize. Indeed, anyone who has lived and worked in a different cultural setting – even newcomers to Canada – will recognize the strands of wonder, confusion, satisfaction and disappointment which make up a cross-cultural experience.

A key ingredient in any such setting is a sense of humor, and Betty Kilgour has a more-than-adequate supply of that essential commodity. She has shared some of it with us in this book.

Chris Bryant
Executive Director
CUSO

Why Africa?

Since, and probably before, I was old enough to comprehend the spoken word, I've heard from various lips in different cadences, "Now why did Betty do that?" To which the people responsible for me at such times would try, often in vain, to explain my action.

In fact, I've often found it a difficult question to answer myself!

I know it is my nature – due possibly to a mixture of Highland Scottish and Tipperary Irish blood in my veins – to explore the unknown, to try what others have failed at or couldn't or wouldn't attempt – usually because of common sense on their part. This love of adventure has played an important part in my tremendous desire to explore other worlds.

As to why Bill and I decided to go to Africa as volunteers, I'm not really sure. I know there was a bit of a wish to help our fellow man, but I'm sure that wasn't the only motive – lofty though it seemed.

Actually, knowing Bill so well and myself even better, it seems only natural or at least plausible that we would one day visit Africa. As a child, I zealously absorbed anything and everything even remotely connected with Africa. I spent hours poring over any book which used the magical word *Africa* as much as four times in three hundred pages.

We lived in small-town Alberta and the whole population practically had to bar me from their personal libraries, I'd pester them so much.

The first movie I ever saw was a war film; the name and actors elude me, but the scenery I'll see forever. It was filmed in northern Africa. I didn't see the blood and guts – I was too busy watching camels, the rolling sands and the odd palm tree.

When I met and married Bill, I discovered I had found not only the man I wanted to spend at least the rest of my life with – I had found my soulmate. His Scottish father, a big game guide and outfitter, had books galore on African explorers and hunters

1

– everything from Teddy Roosevelt's *African Game Trails* to James Corbett. In fact, it was his life-long dream to go to Africa on a safari – a dream which failed to materialize for him but one which Bill adopted as he grew to manhood. But Bill's love of this vast continent was not confined to hunting big game – rather it was the romance of the whole.

We had to be content with movies and books as we built up our farm and raised our five kids; but like a wild oat seed lying dormant, our love of adventure and of Africa lay ready to sprout forth.

One memorable day, we were reading the *Western Producer* and there was an ad placed by CUSO (Canadian University Services Overseas) asking for volunteers for Third-World countries, many in Africa. They were recruiting teachers, doctors, agricultural workers and cattlemen. We certainly knew cattle – we had raised the fool things for thirty years! Our kids were grown, except for Beth who was fourteen at the time, but we could take her with us! Our excitement grew as we discussed it.

Bill attended a recruitment meeting in Calgary and even though he was married, had a child who would travel with us and had no formal training, he did have a wealth of experience in his field.

We were accepted, with a posting in Tanzania, and the wheels were set in motion.

From our first "Let's give it a try" to the final "You've been accepted" there passed not only many agonizing moments ("Have I misplaced my brains?" "Oh, what if we're not accepted?") but also enough letters to paper the Parliament buildings.

Bill and I decided (for a very good reason – we would have been committed) to keep it strictly a secret. But like all good secrets the word leaked out, and each and every time we so much as went to the south forty, some well-meaning soul would confront us.

"What's this we hear? You're selling your farm – how *could* you?" We certainly were not selling anything! Or "How can you leave your little children?" Our "little children" were married and probably glad to be rid of us!

"My goodness, they tell me you won't even have an electric frypan?" Swallowing the urge to scream, "I can fry an egg on a hot rock if I have to!" I started to sneak around, going to town only when I absolutely had to and hiding behind corners when I saw someone with a certain gleam in their eye.

CUSO first began sending volunteers overseas in 1961 and had sent over six thousand of them when we joined the group in 1976. The head office is in Ottawa and it was there that we were sent for our briefing enroute to our posting.

Meanwhile, I had one fine time packing and unpacking, time and time again. Beth, being Beth, a fourteen-year-old tomboy, needed only blue jeans, big shirts and her records. Bill had shirts, jeans and textbooks, but I had to think of clothes for two years, besides all the trappings women have needed since Eve tossed away her fig leaf for Coco Chanel. Besides, I had to remember all the stuff Beth and Bill had scoffed at, which I knew they'd need in due time.

I'm a cold-blooded creature and very seldom suffer from heat – the kids claim I put on mitts to get an ice cube – so I packed for all kinds of weather. But we each had only a 66-pound baggage allowance, which isn't very much once you get started. We didn't know what could be bought in Tanzania so two years' supply of face cream, lipstick and mascara – the necessities – were also hauled along. CUSO supplied each of us with a medical kit containing malaria pills and other needed items, so that was taken care of.

The lists grew longer as the letters flew but we finally had our suitcases packed and we landed in Ottawa.

I found that many of the briefings are staged not to teach facts, but rather to give us a feeling for our host country and to allow us to meet other supposedly sane people embarking on similar adventures. You do learn about the country – the political situation, health aspects, the people and the flora and fauna – but we were really to learn from first-hand experience.

By the time I was briefed on the housing we would enjoy, I (with my too-vivid imagination) could visualize a little white cottage with roses and picket fence. Boy, was I wrong!

Still, we gained a general idea of what we might have to contend with in the way of work, health problems and so on, which gave us a little more self-confidence. We found out we would be flown home if we got sick, died or otherwise caused any trouble.

We were instructed to dress according to the dress code of our host country, to not fool around with politics or drugs and, all in all, do Canada proud!

Away We Go!

The flight seemed long. Not because of lack of comfort – heavens, if there's one thing in this world I love, it's flying. Not the baggage, passport, boarding end of it, but the actual flying time. I think it's the glamor of it all. "Would you like a pillow? White wine or red?" I lap it up like a cow at a salt block!

No, it wasn't the flying time. Rather, I was so anxious to see my beloved Africa.

When we touched down in Nairobi, I was fit to be tied. Bill was busy getting our papers in order and Beth was reading a *Rolling Stone* magazine. I couldn't believe it. Here we were in the Dark Continent of Teddy Roosevelt and Dr. Livingstone and no one was excited but me. It was probably a good thing – one such being aboard a plane was more than enough.

As we disembarked the air was heavy with humidity, and the smell of some tropical flower was strong on the slight breeze. I later learned it was frangipani.

While I was busy oohing and smelling the air, Bill was busy trying to find our two years' worth of baggage. In vain, I might add.

Remembering our departure from London, I recalled a very arrogant Englishman arguing with Bill over this very luggage.

"If you'll get it for me, I'll check it on our flight to Nairobi."

"Hmph. You needn't do that, mate – I'll see to it," he replied, leaning on the counter.

"Yes, but I want to be sure it comes with us," Bill argued.

"Now see here, you're dealing with the British Empire now. When we say your luggage will be there, it will be there!" he puffed. "This is England, not some backward colony!"

But the British Empire let us down; we were on our way to Tanzania with hand baggage and what we had on our backs. Bill carried a radio, my typewriter and a very small shaving kit, Beth her shampoo and pop records and I had my purse which did contain everything but the kitchen sink, and one small carry-all. I had one bottle of duty-free perfume which I had a great use for, as I had to wear the dress I was in for one whole month. That was how long it took the British Empire to get our luggage to us! A few hours later we boarded the smaller Tanzanian Airline plane for our short flight to Dar es Salaam, the capital of Tanzania. We stepped blithely aboard with not a thing to check on.

Enroute, the pilot took a steep bank to the left to show us the peak of Mount Kilimanjaro poking through the clouds. What a sight! I'll never forget it. I left part of my heart there – as well as my stomach – as the pilot banked back onto the flight path.

When we landed in Dar es Salaam we looked about for Kleist Sykes, the field officer who was to meet us. This was to be our first encounter with punctuality in Third-World countries.

I had envisioned being greeted with hearty handshakes, kisses and flowers and being whisked away for a gin and tonic. Surely this was the way of Africa – Rudyard Kipling often spoke of such! So I gazed about looking for a likely man who might just be kissing me in a moment – how exciting! But no one ran forward or even glanced our way.

We found a battered bench and collapsed. It had been a long flight and the bloom was quickly fading from the rose. My head ached, my feet had blistered and puffed over my pumps and the glamor was edging away. Beth just tucked her feet under her and went to sleep. I finally retreated to the rest room and took off my pantyhose, never to don them again till we left for home two years later.

I began to stew. "Bill, what if we've landed in Uganda or something? Maybe we got our days mixed up!" Bill finally told me to be quiet and he went for a stroll. But about an hour later, in came a tall, slender, handsome Tanzanian who sauntered over to us.

"You wouldn't happen to be the Kilgours, would you?" It was a dumb question. The only others in the whole building were two little kids tossing dice and a fat official snoozing at a desk.

"Why, yes, we are!"

"Sorry I'm late. I was up to my neck in paperwork and the

time just slipped away." That was our introduction to Kleist. I was later to notice that the field officials were up to their necks in paperwork because they never did it. You could barely see the tops of their desks at any time, busy or not.

Anyway, we all climbed into Kleist's little car and dashed like a crazed wildebeest through the streets of Dar. These streets all run every which way with the odd English roundabout here and there. To cross a street in Dar, you put your life on the line and run like the very devil to the centre, then make another mad dash across the remaining half. Tanzanians drive on the opposite side of the street, too, which adds to the excitement. By the time we got to the airliner hotel, my hair was trying to stand on end but was too limp to do so.

Dar es Salaam (in Arabic, "haven of peace") is still very English in manner, especially the hotels. It was like stepping into the old colonial world. There were fans whirring, mosquito nets about the beds and jugs of lime juice on the stands.

I plopped on the bed after seeing Beth ensconced next door and checking her room for critters and crawlies. Bill and Kleist were discussing plans for the next day, but I was so pooped by then, all I wanted was to die a peaceful death.

But after a good sleep we all felt better. Supper, or dinner as we learned to call our evening meal, was our first in our new country and I lapped up the attention from our white-coated waiters.

That evening, when we stepped outside, we were amazed to find it as hot as the afternoon. I don't think the temperature dropped a degree. We were treated to a tour of the main part of Dar by Lucille Blundt. Lucille was an older lady, a volunteer from Canada who had been teaching in Dar for years. She loved it so much she kept extending and extending, and finally married a Tanzanian who was in charge of the Coca-Cola company in Dar.

Lucille had more common sense than a lot and was very down-to-earth. She toured us about, tossing in odd bits of helpful information – how to barter, what to pay for a taxi, and how to fend off pedlars. But the whole thing was so disorienting to me at the time, I couldn't think of a thing to ask except whether I could buy Tampax in Sumbawanga! (I couldn't.)

I fell asleep that night, the whir of the huge fan over our heads and crickets chirping somewhere as my lullaby.

Tanzania

Tanzania, the country where we spent two wonderful years, is different. It is relatively untouched in many areas, as far as tourism goes.

James Mellon, in his book *African Hunter*, called it uncouth – but to me it's rather like a sprawling country cousin of Kenya. Tanzania has a beauty all its own – rustic, remote, free and wild. It seems to be the one country left in which the Africa of old carries on like an island by itself – the old tribal Africa.

It's the only country that still has corners where you can go out on safari as in the old days.

The roads are dreadful, except for a few main highways, and it takes hours to go even a few miles. They are full of holes, hard in the dry season and muddy in wet season. In the backwoods you can mire down in foot-deep elephant tracks and often you have to lay planks here and there just to get through. You can very easily total a brand-new Land Rover in a year of use. You bend springs, shear bolts and wreck shock absorbers – not to mention the bruises and bumps your own body absorbs. That's why the country is the Africa of old.

Britain granted Tanganyika independence in 1961. In 1964 the United Republic of Tanzania was formed by the union of Tanganyika and Zanzibar, with the name Tanzania adopted on October 29th, 1964. Julius Nyerere as president certainly was the man of the hour for this struggling new nation, and went on to become well-respected by the other African nations and indeed by the whole world.

The area of the mainland is approximately 362,700 square miles, with 20,000 square miles of inland waters. It is bordered on the east by the Indian Ocean, on the north by Kenya, Lake Victoria and Uganda, on the west by Rwanda, Burundi and Lake Tanganyika (on the other side of the lake lies Zaire), and on the south by Zambia, Malawi and Mozambique.

Lake Tanganyika is the world's second-deepest freshwater lake, and Tanzania's Mount Kilimanjaro is Africa's highest mountain.

The climate varies and is not typically tropical. Rainfall can be anywhere from 14 inches to 123 inches a year. There are three climatic zones: the hot, humid coastal area, the drier central plateau and the semi-temperate mountain areas. Actually Tanzania is cool in the dry season – at Sumbawanga where we were posted, it's like Alberta in June a great deal of the time.

The largest portion of the country's African population is composed of over one hundred tribes of the Bantu-speaking groups. There is a substantial community of people originally from India who are referred to as Asian and who have immigrated to East Africa during the last three centuries, but mostly since 1900. Arab immigrants and others of Persian origin have been settling in East Africa for at least a thousand years.

On the mainland there are some 120 tribes. Swahili is the official language and the main religions are Islam, Roman Catholicism and Protestantism.

Our headquarters was a government ranch at Sumbawanga – Sumbawanga, I was later to learn, is the Siberia of Tanzania. If an official gets into trouble he is banished to Sumbawanga!

Much of Tanzania is riddled with the tsetse fly, which continues to hinder livestock breeding, but modern science is slowly ridding the country of this pest.

Tanzania is a big-game hunter's and camera buff's paradise in both variety and quantity of game. More game animals roam within its borders than in any other country in the world.

There's a relatively rich diamond mine, the history of which I enjoyed. A Canadian, sometime in the early 1900s, was out strolling and stopped to visit some natives who were playing a game with what he thought were pebbles. To his great astonishment, on looking closer he saw that they were huge diamonds! I was told there's a statue dedicated to this gentleman in Dar today. The mine was sold to DeBeers, one of the largest diamond companies in the world.

At Uvinza there's a large salt mine, but ironically, anytime I was in Uvinza I couldn't buy a grain of salt!

Will I Ever Learn Swahili?

Our next stop after staying overnight in Dar was upcountry at Morogoro, where we stayed at a teachers' training college while attending language classes.

This college was situated four miles out of town and was nestled in a hillside, surrounded by flowering shrubs. Behind the college was a real rain forest and above it, cliffs with mica slabs. I was later to remember seeing mica used as the windows in the old-time heaters of pioneer days in Canada.

At this college we were placed in dorms along with our fellow classmates from various lands who also were there to learn Swahili. There were many countries represented. One man from England was to take over the British volunteer service in Dar as Field Staff Officer. Another was a big brusque fellow from the Netherlands who had worked in many African countries and had pictures of his female conquests in each one – some quite beautiful, and some – well, beauty is in the eye of the beholder, it's said!

The college was guarded by soldiers, and this fellow would go into town several times a week to visit the various bars, getting back in the wee small hours. He was usually quite inebriated and when challenged by the guards, who didn't care to let him by, he'd invariably start bellowing.

"I'm here out of the goodness of my heart to help you poor buggers and look at the thanks I get! Keep me from my bed, will you!" And the long-suffering guards would send him on in until the next night, when the whole charade would be re-enacted.

The Swahili classes were a disaster as far as I was concerned. Beth picked it up quickly and easily. Bill was not too bad (I think he bluffed a bit) but I just couldn't learn a thing – which was a dreadful blow to my ego. I had always prided myself on being excellent at memory work at school. I could learn all my lines for a two-hour play in just a few days, but I just could not master even the basics of Swahili. Of course anyone who, after two years of school French, knew but one French phrase – "Shut your mouth!" – should not have been expecting to learn much

Swahili in three weeks!

Another reason I was extra dull – I couldn't stay awake. Not just in class, mind you, but when special speakers would arrive after lunch to fulminate on various subjects, I'd fall fast asleep. I'd try all sorts of ways to stay awake – I'd pinch the inner part of my thigh and bite my lip, but to no avail. This really embarrassed Beth and me, but it just about finished Bill off. At this particular time he was wishing he were a dashing young bachelor, and not tied to a fourteen-year-old kid and a wife who couldn't stay awake.

Probably I was still suffering from jet lag, and I know I was extra tired, as the months before had been so hectic. Anyway, for the whole three weeks I fought this ailment. Finally, Bill sent me, like a wayward child, to our room if a speaker arrived. Of course, in all honesty, most of the speakers were dull and long-winded and always political. So instead of being bored I slept! But I know I left more than one speaker with a bad case of doubt in his powers as a great orator.

It was in the little town of Morogoro that we had our first real glimpse of the other side of Africa – the Africa of poverty, the lepers who were cured but still bore the horrible scars of the disease. Many had limbs and parts of their faces missing, and were reduced to begging at the street corners. I had wondered as I first saw them if I could ever overcome my sense of horror, but you see a lot of Hansen's disease in Dar, and I learned to drop shillings in their hands without a quiver.

It was here we had our first view of the African market – the colors, the smells – as well as the little *dukas* which became an important part of life over the next two years.

Beth and I would haunt the dukas (the local equivalent of a corner store), for what, we were never sure. One time Beth had wandered off and I heard her shout, "Mom, look!" It was a "Mom, look!" that she would let fly whenever she had spied something very wonderful, so I tore over. It turned out to be a real Mars bar in a dusty jar. We paid twenty shillings for it (about three dollars!) but we agreed it was worth it. We'd save it for our evening snack – Beth fairly drooled in anticipation. But the gods were not with us. When she opened it, our lovely treat was wrinkled, dried, white and dusty – and hard as a rock. I flung it in disgust at the wall, and all it did was bounce. (Of course, we were not starving. The food was excellent and the market was full of all sorts of fruits, papayas, bananas of all kinds, and pineapples.) Looking back now, I see that our month at the school prepared us for the way of life we were soon to lead. Sort of like placing month-old chicks in a separate pen before tossing them into the flock. So even if the language lessons were a waste of time, the month as a whole was certainly worthwhile.

It was during our last week at the college that our luggage finally arrived. You can imagine the excitement. We had forgotten what we had packed and oh, the joy of getting into some fresh clothes. All was in order but one kit bag of Bill's. It had contained his good camera and all the lenses and stuff his family had bought for him every Christmas, birthday and Father's Day for years back. And his denim jacket. So we were left with my camera, a very basic one with no trimmings. You couldn't put any attachments on it even if you could have bought them. All I had ever used it for was black-and-white pictures to illustrate articles, and I certainly was no photographer. But beggars can't be choosers and Bill, rather sheepishly I'll admit, laid claim to it.

At Morogoro, too, we had our first glimpse of Tanzanian buses. If you are the tiniest blt claustrophobic you'll understand Bill's horror! He told us emphatically that we could travel anywhere we wanted, but nothing, absolutely nothing, could persuade him to climb on one of those buses! I could understand his dismay. The buses were packed to the very brim and flowing over. People were sitting on top of each other, filling the aisles, hanging out the windows and on the outside hanging on. The baggage was tossed on top and the bus would go careening along and on occasion when it slowed for a corner, someone would leap onto the step or through an open window. Of course Bill did ride on those buses, as did we all, and as with so many other situations, we learned to cope and even became quite inured to it all.

A-Shopping We Will Go!

There's nothing, but nothing, that cheers the cockles of my heart like being handed a wad of money and being told to go spend it. But that's what happened when we got back to Dar. CUSO might have allowed us very little in the way of baggage, but they more than made up for it with a substantial settling-in allowance. Of course, we had literally nothing in the way of household goods, even the basics. I had tucked in a good butcher knife, my sewing shears, a couple of towels and Bill's alarm clock, but other than that we were bereft. So we sat in the hotel lobby over juice and made lists. Imagine trying to make lists when all you have is a butcher knife and sewing shears! Pots, pans, utensils, bedding – Lord, what a job!

There are many strange sights in the streets of Dar, but it took the populace a while to get used to seeing the strange *mzungu* (whites) marching around, lugging everything from pillows to pots for a whole week. It was fun, though. We'd shop like crazy all day, then have a leisurely shower and dinner at our hotel. Waiters with white towels over their arms would glide about, tending to our every whim, inquiring about our success that particular day. Beth was treated like the little princess she was, in her blue jeans which every African covets, and her long brown hair which they'd touch every chance they got. She could also sass the urchins back in Swahili, which placed her a step above the rest of us.

One purchase we made, which was very important to me, was a sewing machine. How else would I mend Bill's jeans – and this did prove to be one of our wisest buys. The cost of a treadle machine was beyond reason so we settled for a little one you ran by turning a crank on the wheel. It was a portable – that is, if you were strong enough to lift it. I wasn't sure how I'd be able to sew and turn the crank at the same time but by that time, I had a worse crank to contend with – what is it about shopping that turns a usually charming man into an old goat?

Then I had to buy enough material to justify the purchase of the sewing machine – bolts and bolts of it. I didn't have a clue what windows would need curtains, and being from the old school – better safe than sorry – I bought enough to drape Balmoral Castle.

Soon the week had passed and we were to leave for Sumbawanga. At five the alarm went off and Bill was up, whistling away. We had packed as much as possible the night before and had even loaded a lot into the Land Rover, with the driver sleeping in it overnight so nothing would walk away!

Beth and I started hauling bags and boxes downstairs to Bill who loaded them, and after three or four trips we began to wonder how on earth we'd get in after it was loaded. The driver assigned by NARCO was a droll little chap in a tattered shirt, red thongs and a knitted toque, just like the kids wore in the winter. This was a brilliant pink one with a great white tassel, and he wore it with pride. By then I was used to weird get-ups and he looked just fine in his red thongs and woman's hat!

After much poking and grunting, the loaded Land Rover was more or less roadworthy, with the odd thing hanging out the window and the spare tire on top of it all, holding it down.

By the time the sun broke over the horizon we were away. Our plan was to get to Sumbawanga by nightfall – a trip, I was later to find, which took me two to three days each time I travelled it. But ignorance is bliss and we were all in high spirits.

The rear seat was so packed, there was room for only one passenger, so I, being clever, decided I could catch a bit of sleep if I sat back there. So I offered – just a bit piously – to let the others view the scenery from the front. I smirked to myself and let out a groan or two for effect and settled back for a rest.

There's nothing as lovely as an early-morning drive upcountry in Tanzania. The first part of the trip was over hard surface so with just the odd bump we sailed right along. Our route took us through a large game reserve and we were fortunate to see plentiful game. First the ungainly wildebeest which, to me, looks like a cross between a horse and an angry moose. We were treated to a good look at a giraffe, which is my favorite of all animals. The plains were at times absolutely packed with antelope of all kinds, mixed together with the little "bad boys," the zebra. Farther along we were forced to stop while two elephants decided whether to cross the highway or visit in the centre.

I've had many people ask, "Weren't you afraid?" when hearing about one of our many adventures; but speaking for myself, I can only say "No." When we arrived there, it was as if we had been placed on another planet and so the normal fears of an Alberta housewife just did not apply. I do know that at home, if I saw an earthworm on my garden glove I'd have a fit. But in Africa I could (and did) meet elephants, snakes and all sorts of other creatures and didn't bat an eye.

By the time we had passed through the game reserve I was begging for a front seat, but to no avail. "You wanted the rear one, kiddo – you've got it!"

We stopped at a little roadside duka for some bananas and roasted groundnuts and to have a bit of a stretch. Farther on we pulled over to go to the bathroom – the bathroom being the wide open plains with a bush to duck behind. Beth and I were still a bit shy about these matters, but we whistled and hummed to keep our courage up and to scare away anything that might be hiding near the bush we picked. We had good reason to make this racket: we had heard a scary story in Dar about this outdoor style of bathroom. It seems two CUSO volunteers were on their way to their new posting and their bus stopped to let the passengers out for bathroom privileges. Everybody filed off, and when one big lady squatted behind a bush, a snake bit her bottom and she died instantly! They had to bring her body back onto the bus to complete the journey to her home village. It was enough to scare off even the most zealous volunteer!

The heat of the day was upon us by the time we arrived in Iringa for lunch. We were stiff, sore and hungry and the little hotel beckoned to us like a cool oasis. Of course, for any tourist used to Hilton hotels it would have seemed a sad affair, but we pride ourselves on coping easily "when in Rome." So anything I didn't have to prepare myself was fine with me. I was used to cobwebs and geckos by now, and was mighty pleased to have lunch served. The place had a rustic charm all its own, with open-beam ceiling and cement floor. I learned during my stay in

Africa (short though it had been thus far) that you never, to save your sanity as well as your breakfast, look in the kitchen of a guest house or small hotel.

We were soon satisfied and off once more. But this half of the trip was not to be a pleasant experience. We had run out of hard surface, it was hot and we were tired.

We took turns sitting in the back. The road was rougher than the cow pasture at home, often with huge rocks and great gaping holes. The red dust filtered around us and the spare tire kept slipping forward and whopping me on the head. The Land Rover, which had been fine on the good highway, seemed to lose its springs and shock absorbers and we felt like we were riding a wheelbarrow full of bolts.

The driver kept repeating, "It's rough 'cause the Mama has too much stuff," to which Bill would heartily agree.

Bill and I have only a few real disagreements besides what I do with money. What I carry on trips is a big one. He's from the old, sensible, typical man's school – you carry what you take, so you go light. Over the years I seem to have spent a great deal of time begging him to help. "Carry just this one bag, honey!" I'd plead, to which he'd growl something, usually not fit for tender ears. The one big fight I remember happened in England. I was loaded to the eyeballs with gifts for our kids and we were just getting on a train. I felt he could at least help carry something – they were for *his* kids too – but no way. Here I am with three heavy suitcases and he with one. Does he help me? Hah! But as I look about, here he is assisting a well-stacked brassy blond carrying one shopping bag onto the train. The fat hit the fire! He kept insisting she was old and crippled and I'd snort, "Crippled! *Top heavy* you mean!"

The day progressed and only those who have travelled African roads can appreciate my story. We were shaken apart by the time we reached our destination that night at ten. I had planned on making a decent impression at the ranch but by that time I could barely walk, never mind make a grand entrance at the ranch manager's home. His wife told us her husband was in town and not only wasn't our house painted and ready, it was still occupied.

Beth and I were so tired we were numb. We were driven into the little town where we were installed in what they call a guest house. As it turned out, there were several in town that were quite okay but they were all closed and barred for the night. The one still open was the very worst in the whole town. It was dreadful! Like Beth said, "It's a real *crud*, Dad!" But we had no choice.

I got Beth settled, muttered at Bill, "How could you?" and collapsed. I left all my clothes on and stuck my big purse under my head. For some insane reason I was lugging around a pure wool cape which I draped over myself. But sleep evaded me. I'd just doze off and some noise would wake me. Positive someone was lurking outside and about to do what I don't know, I'd pretend I was talking to someone so they'd be too scared to attempt to break in. I was *so* glad when morning arrived. I thought I'd go for a wash but I found there wasn't a bathroom. The toilet was a hole in the ground with three walls around it.

Those twenty-four hours were my real orientation class. This was the final test. The weeks at Morogoro were nothing – this was my testing ground and cope I did! This was the Africa of magnificent beauty and untold squalor that I was to work in for two years!

Later that day we were moved to a clean, nice guest house, the other episode being the very lowest of the low of our two years there. After a good wash, a sleep and a little tour of the town we felt so much better. It was probably a good thing we had hit bottom that night, as everything seemed absolutely cushy after that experience.

We stayed at the guest house for a week while our house was being prepared and we began to get the feel of the people and the area.

Our New Home

When our house was ready we moved out to the ranch. It was a joyful day for me, as well as the end of our long, long journey.

The government ranch which was to be our headquarters was about twelve miles out of town. The house was nestled near the top of Malonje hill, over seven thousand feet above sea level. Far below lay a great African plain, like burnished gold in the dry season, and green and alive with new growth in the rainy season.

From our patio you could see the *bomas* (corrals) and in the morning and early evening when the cattle were herded to and from them, it seemed as though the whole valley was alive and moving. It was a magnificent view and I fell in love with it at first sight.

Our home was lovely in a rustic, run-down manner, like an old duchess down on her luck. But it must have been a real showplace when first constructed. It had been built by a German family by the name of Damm, who had owned the ranch before independence, and around the name of Damm whirled many stories – whether all true or not, I'll never know. But usually where there's smoke, there's fire, and some of the stories were so dreadful I don't see how anyone could have made them up.

The Damms had many cattle and employed Tanzanians to work as laborers, herdsmen and gardeners – all to help the family build its little empire. The villagers nearby as well as the employed workers lived in mortal fear of these people. I was told by various people that the Damms frequently used whips on the natives, and set their dogs on them. In their eyes, the natives were subhuman.

One time I was visiting a friend in town, and she and I stepped out to see something in her garden. As we stood there chatting, a little village mama came along, basket atop her head. She glanced over, spotted me and let out a shriek that would wake the dead. The basket went flying as she tore off ninety miles an hour down the dusty road. You would have thought the very devil was at her heels – which I later found out she thought I was. My friend cornered her the next day and learned that the lady thought I was Mrs. Damm, returned to plague them once more. Needless to say I didn't take it as a compliment!

Mr. Damm deserted his wife and went to Moshi where he bought a coffee farm. He was later murdered there and the culprits were never caught. Mrs. Damm and the kids stayed on, with her eldest son living where the ranch manager lived while we were there. I gather the lady kept right on as before and was loathed and feared the same. She was so hated that one night, some workers dragged a huge boulder up the side of the house and rolled it in the bedroom window smack on top of her bed. But wouldn't you know it – that night she had felt chilly and had slept in the bed across the room! I can't help but think the natives hated her with great passion – those walls were fifteen feet high!

The last seen of Mrs. Damm was when Tanzania got its independence and, figuring her number was up, she herded all her cattle on foot and headed for the Zambian border.

It's funny, though. The natives who rolled the stone onto her bed were the same ones who were so protective towards Beth and me. Bill was away three quarters of the time, and even Beth was at school for three months at a stretch so I was usually alone. But I never locked my bedroom door, not feeling the need to. One night I was awakened about two o'clock by footsteps around my house. I listened, wondering who on earth it was. I finally got up, found my flashlight and crept out to see what was going on, my heart in my mouth. As I shone the dim light about, I heard a voice. "Never mind, Mama Beth, it's only me – Michael. I am watching over you!" Michael was the night watchman who always stopped for tea on his way to turn on the power generator at night.

Our house was a huge brick and stone affair with funny little rooms stuck on the outside corners like afterthoughts – possibly for the new child in the family or a visiting relative. The walls were a good foot thick and kept everything out, including the heat. The main floor consisted of two huge rooms divided by a magnificent fireplace, all tiled with ceramic tiles in the German style. When we moved in, the tiles housed more cockroaches and in more sizes than you can imagine. But with a good scouring with disinfectant and lots of hot fires, we finally got rid of the pests.

The fireplace could be used from either the living room or the dining room, and had little benches built in so you could sit and enjoy the fire. (Even if they have the proper tools, which is rare, the natives don't chop the wood to fit the fireplace – they just bring the whole trunk in and lay one end in the fire with the rest stretched across the room. As the end burns, they just shove it farther in until the whole log is burned. Then they look for another tree.) Bill bought an axe and we did chop the wood, but we also found the old husks from the maize harvest were wonderful for starting the fire and making a quick, very hot blaze.

Our furniture was basic government issue but was quite comfortable: wooden-framed chairs and couch with thick foam pads for cushions, basic table, chairs and old iron-framed single cots for beds. There were huge windows made up of dozens of tiny panes of glass. There was a little propane stove which had three burners but of course there were great spells when the supply of propane would run out and I'd be forced to do my cooking on little single-burner Chinese hot plates – this took a bit of talent, I can tell you!

The floors were all cement because of the insect problem, but the villagers in the area wove beautiful mats. These I tossed here and there, which gave the house a homey look, besides helping to cushion the feet for standing for any length of time.

There was also a little, very dark back kitchen, but it was so dismal that I cooked in the dining room, using the kitchen for storing stuff.

The upstairs was approached from the outside, where giant stone steps took you to the two bedrooms. The Damms must have had awfully long legs – I practically had to take a run at those steps, they were so far apart. Coming down was a different matter. I always had the old childhood urge to sit and skin down on my bottom.

The bathroom was yet another little room which boasted an

outside entrance. Actually it didn't have much to boast of – a bedraggled old tub and a very small sink, sometimes with running water, sometimes not. There was also one window which had three panes of glass missing. Mr. Mbani promised it would be fixed before the week was out, but anyone familiar with Africa will understand when I say it was still broken when our two-year term was up.

The broken window wasn't all bad, though. I had planted some nasturtium seeds in the planter at the front door. The seeds came from Bowden, Alberta but they loved the Sumbawanga climate. The silly things went nuts, climbing up the twelve-foot brick wall, around the corner and up through the broken bathroom window. To make the story even better, one day I went in the bathroom and there, perched on a blossom, was a little yellow bird singing his heart out. Now if Mbani had seen to repairs, I'd have missed that experience!

I also planted some Evening Scented Stock which grew prolifically and smelled heavenly each evening. My favorite spot after a hard day was on the little brick seat on the patio listening to the creatures of the night with the lovely scent of Stock wafting by on the evening breeze.

Besides the main part of the house, there were the other little rooms tacked onto various corners of the house. They were handy for storing the sacks of wheat I'd sometimes keep for grinding when there were flour shortages. These rooms were also handy for guests. In fact, at times I'd have guests I didn't know about, only seeing them if I glanced out early in the morning. It was quite commonplace to see a couple of ladies or old men sneaking off down the hill in the early light. Prosper, my houseboy, would often ask permission for his wife's relatives to bunk overnight if they came from a far village. At first I'd change the cots, putting on my best sheets and blankets, but I soon found the guests would fold up all my stuff and roll up in their own blankets. Whether they thought I wasn't that great a housekeeper or they didn't trust Western bedding, I never found out.

Along with our old house, I also acquired Francis. A chum of Prosper's, Francis was living in a back bedroom of the house when we moved in, so in exchange for board and room, it was decided he would coach us in Swahili. He was a very gentle quiet boy, in direct contrast to Prosper's noisy exuberance, and he assisted the mechanic at the ranch. (The Swahili lessons petered out in a couple of months, but the friendship remained right to the end.)

We had water piped in, but to heat it there was a gigantic drum at the back with a firepit under it. When I needed hot water I'd have Prosper start the fire and fill the drum. This would give us enough water for baths and a bit to wash clothes with, although Prosper preferred to wash in cold water.

As time went on I got out my great bolts of material and made covers for the cushions and bright drapes and, with the woven mats and pictures from magazines stuck on the walls, the old house took on a warm, cosy character.

The weather was chilly in the dry season and usually a wind blew every night, lulling us to sleep. I normally had the fireplace going at least a bit each day to take the chill off, but we were over seven thousand feet above sea level so it was quite dry. Being part of the Great Rift valley we were treated, one might say, to a mild earthquake at least once a month. (These frequent earthquakes were barely noticed, even when they were severe enough to sit you down. Thunder and lightning were rare, however, and the people were quite afraid of them.)

I'll remember forever our first night in our home. I had a hard time sleeping – my mind running wild with the weird and wonderful middle-of the-night thoughts that accompany the start of an incredible adventure. By morning I was still wide awake and I rose early to see the countryside wake up.

I ran downstairs and pulled back the drapes to soak in the beauty of the vast plain below. To my utter astonishment, instead of a great lovely view, each little pane of glass held a little ebony face. Some jumped back and others just grinned – they had come to see the *mzungu*, like our kids would go to see a circus. I never found out what they thought of me – I only know I felt weird. I tried to pretend they weren't there; I went about my morning chores but I felt like a grade C actress who didn't know her part. I went upstairs and came back in half an hour, thinking they would be gone – no luck. If anything, there were more of them. This was to be repeated every day for a whole week – Beth became totally nocturnal. After that it was only visitors who came for a look. There was a bank partway up the hill which provided a perfect seating arrangement for visitors, and many times I'd go about my work with an audience.

As the days sped by, Beth and I explored the ranch headquarters. The offices, our home and the manager's house were near the top of Melenji hill. Walking up the hill was a real hike and took at least twenty minutes. Along with the houses and offices, we found an old swimming pool. It was quite large, but was completely hidden by overgrowth. I'm sure it could have been restored to its original condition but the ranch manager didn't see the need for such a thing as a swimming pool. And any Tanzanians I knew had other things on their minds – like figuring out where the next meal was coming from.

We also found, amidst the growth on our little terraced garden, real English roses and lovely calla lilies. These thrived once we had cleared the weeds away and dug around them, letting in the sun and freeing the roots.

Down near the offices we found a little duka which sold odds and ends – cooking oil, kerosene, plastic thongs and on the odd occasion, sugar and margarine. Mixed in with these staples were strange items that one can only wonder about. Beth, on digging around, came upon tins and tins of sweetened condensed milk that must have been there for eons. The Africans who could afford these tins didn't buy them, simply because they didn't have a clue what they were. We bought them dirt-cheap and ate the contents by the spoonful.

Housekeeping was certainly different than what I was used to, even on a busy Alberta farm. I really roughed it in many ways, although this certainly didn't bother me. There was no fridge, no vacuum, no mixer – not even an egg beater. I could use the electric iron only when the generator was switched on from seven-thirty until ten at night. But I could borrow Joyce's charcoal iron, which really heated better than the electric one. I fought the little sugar ants constantly. You could not leave the smallest crumb of food anywhere or there would be a trail of little ants to it in a matter of minutes.

But I was far less fussy in Africa than I am at home – and I'm not all that fussy here! It was like stepping back into pioneer days, I'm sure, and I found it challenging and, more than once, hilarious.

Our old German-style house atop the high hill at our headquarters, seen from the corral below.

Typical countryside near Lake Tanganyika.

Bill with one of the many forms of wildlife found at Uvinza!

Patients waiting for me to open the clinic early in the morning.

A typical Tanzanian village.

Prosper and Queenie. He was a proud papa!

Prosper

There was a rule in our contract – whether written or not I never found out – which stated we were to hire househelp, wanted or not, and pay a decent wage for it. "Good public relations," we were told.

So Prosper arrived and our lives were never quite the same again.

Prosper was a stocky village boy, about twenty, with a grin that lit his face like the Eternal Flame. He had never worked for whites before; in fact, he had never worked as a houseboy before. But he had a burning ambition to cook for a great hotel like the Agip in Dar, and as he didn't lack for self-confidence, he was ready to take on anything I threw at him. Many times thereafter I *did* feel like throwing things at him, I might add.

On a farm in Alberta the woman does her own housework and often a good bit of the outside chores as well, taking great pride in these accomplishments. The only help I ever had on our farm was a lady to look after meals and kids while I had yet another baby – and these ladies, much as I loved them, were sent packing as soon as I could run my home once more.

Not that I minded someone scrubbing those cement floors – I'm not that proud, or stupid! I simply didn't know how to boss someone. I can just hear my family groaning over that remark, but it was true. I had this inborn thing about working right alongside Prosper which really bothered him. I'd be knee-deep in cleaning and Prosper would shake his head. "Mama, you must not do this. What will people think?" No self-respecting mama would scrub and clean – it just wasn't done!

Of course Prosper wasn't really sure quite what to do with me either. Besides, taking orders from a white woman was just a bit much in his eyes. So with a great deal of misunderstanding and very often mayhem, we got along just fine.

Prosper's jobs were to keep the house clean, heat the water, wash the clothes by hand and whatever else I needed done. The floors he'd wash every second day, usually before I was up.

He'd get down on his knees with a bucket of water and an old gunny sack and scrub zealously, but somehow he never got closer to the wall than twenty inches. Then, with great relish, he'd dump the whole bucket over the floor to rinse it, splashing dirty water halfway up the calcimined walls. About once a month after he left for the day, I'd get out an old pot cleaner and some hot soapy water and go around the edges, always keeping an eye out for Prosper or one of his cronies.

The windows were huge but were divided into twelve dozen little panes of glass. These were always dusty and usually smudged with little handprints. Prosper would be really annoyed with me if I started cleaning them, but his idea of cleaning a window and mine were completely opposite. I might add here that there were very few windows in the village huts, and these had no glass in them to clean. (In fact, even the Tanzanians I knew in town who had windows would hang their drapes with the pattern facing out so passersby would enjoy them, the inhabitants just viewing seams from the inside!)

Prosper would wipe these panes with a dirty rag and an old newspaper – but just in the centre; so when the visibility was reduced to an opening about the size of a fifty-cent piece, I'd proceed to clean them myself.

Prosper loved to cook and was really good at it – especially the Tanzanian basics. But he wanted me to teach him my recipes. One thing he did become quite good at was a plain butter cake, but we had so many shortages – eggs, sugar and margarine – that our real lessons were few and far between.

If we had dinner guests I'd instruct Prosper on the finer points of serving guests and let him cook at least one special dish. But he seemed to need an extra drink of pombi at such times – possibly to bolster his confidence. More than one of our guests would frown and wonder why I didn't get a better house-boy, but we were novices, Prosper and I, and we were busy learning together.

I planned a big dinner party one night. I had saved some jelly powder from home along with some other goodies, and invited about fifteen people. This group was a real mixture: two

Catholic priests, one a Frenchman and one German, Helge and Liv, our Norwegian friends, a German girl who was teaching in town, as well as others. I had *worked* at this gala. White lace cloth, linen serviettes and even food! But Prosper must have been overwhelmed by the whole affair, as he came in reeling. As the evening progressed, the noise from the back kitchen – pots dropping, doors banging and off-key whistling – was not to be believed. He'd slosh each course rather than serve it, and by the time coffee was served he was doing a little tribal dance as he poured. (I later found his empty bottle of courage hidden behind a cabbage head.)

Prosper loved to be sent on errands – to the villages to try and buy an egg or two, a chicken, or possibly some potatoes, or to town to buy groceries. He'd catch a ride in at nine o'clock with the ranch Land Rover and wouldn't get back till six or seven at night, with precious few groceries and of course no shillings. But I could always depend on a good healthy yarn.

The odd time, just to save my sanity, I'd send him off on some errand to a village six or seven miles away.

Sometimes when I was sewing he'd stand by my side and turn the crank on my little machine while we discussed issues of great importance: who's the new witch at the ranch, who had a new batch of pombi brewing and what to do with Mama Queenie – his wife.

Mama Queenie was a stolid, dull village girl who was forever giving Prosper grief. He was always having to keep their little one-year-old, and Mama Queenie was always mad about something. One night four truckers arrived at the ranch, and by golly, Mama Queenie slept with the whole works at once – so there must have been more energy there than what showed on the surface. This time, Prosper was the mad one – his outrage was magnificent. It took three days and Mr. Idi the butcher to settle the affair!

Prosper always had an eye out for ways to make money and he eyed my little sewing machine with great interest. One night he asked if he could take it home for two days. I had visions of my machine being taken apart to see what made it work so I said no, but he could use it at my house anytime his chores were all finished. He gave me a great extended bow and began to build up a lucrative business mending clothes for the workers — with my thread and patches! When our term was up we gave Prosper the machine and the last time I saw him was as he sauntered down a dusty village lane, machine under his arm — thinking, no doubt, of his next adventure.

Joyce

One of my first guests was Joyce Mbani, the ranch manager's wife, and she was to become my dearest friend while we lived on the ranch.

The morning Joyce made her official call she was dressed to the hilt – a thing Joyce could do with great style. A tiny lady, barely five feet tall with child-size hands and wrists and size three feet, she was dressed in her little shift dress with her best *kanga* tied about her waist. Her head was adorned with a great turban made of another kanga and she wore her latest shoes – Batas, orange and red ones. She carried a little jar of sugar as a welcome gift – I was soon to find out what a treasure sugar was at Sumbawanga.

Joyce, in my eyes, was really the queen of the area. She was cultured, had gone to school – and besides, she owned thirty-six kangas! The kanga, I should explain, is an item of social status – the more you own, the higher up you are on the social ladder. It's a length of cloth about two yards long, and is the basic garment of the native women. If you have money, a little shift dress or a blouse is worn underneath. It is tied in various ways, around the middle over the shift, above the bosom if not, or in some areas they go bare-breasted still. The kanga is very versatile, though – or maybe it's the ladies who are – anyway, they can twist and roll the kanga into the most beautiful of hats, they use it as a sling on their backs for their babies and they can roll it another way to make a cushion to set baskets on when carrying them on their heads. Joyce also used hers for a tablecloth if she had visitors from town. The kangas made in Tanzania were very colorful but the cotton was not as fine-quality as that from Kenya or Zambia. Tanzania did bring out new patterns four or five times a year, many commemorating various happenings in the country.

Joyce had three children, a girl and two boys. Lkanga, a beautiful boy with soft Bambi eyes, had to be the most handsome child I had ever seen. He had a gentlemanly manner and was always taking charge of situations. He loved being in the limelight. One time Joyce gave him a few shillings to go to the ranch duka and buy a little package of cookies. After waiting half an hour she came down to my house to see where he was. We found Lkanga out on our patio handing out cookies to all and sundry, smiling beatifically like they were manna from heaven. Joyce wasn't impressed; poor Lkanga was hauled off rather unceremoniously by the ear, clutching the now-empty cookie box.

Then there was Mnaco and he was as full of the devil as his brother was angelic. He got away with a great deal. A little pot-bellied urchin, he'd tease and tease and when his poor mother would grab the switch, he'd tear down the hill and hide behind me, laughing all the way, knowing full well that if he made it to me, he was safe.

Mnaco was afraid of me only once – all because of my poor command of Swahili. I was busy at my desk, with little Mnaco playing by my feet. I felt a bit chilly and told Prosper in Swahili to throw some more wood on the fire – or so I thought.

Suddenly Mnaco's eyes widened in terror and he ran screeching out the back door and up the hill. Poor Prosper was laughing so hard he was doubled right over, and it was a good five minutes before he could contain himself long enough to tell me what was wrong. Instead of saying *wood*, I had told Prosper to throw the *kid* on the fire! It took at least eight hours and a bag of candy to convince Mnaco to forgive me.

Mary, the eldest, was six or seven but was so introverted my heart ached for her. Many days I'd go into my living room for something or other and find Mary there, sitting quiet as a mouse. Mary was raised harshly as are most Tanzanian girls. Mothers feel that a woman's role is a hard one, which is very true, so they try to raise their daughters accordingly. They are taught to work hard from a very early age, with little encouragement and never a cuddle or a kiss. Most of the girls were tough enough to handle this treatment but Mary was too sensitive, and so she retreated into herself, never speaking one word to her mother. Joyce was worried about this – a girl should talk to her mother! But she couldn't understand when I tried to explain that Mary needed love and affection more than the boys.

Joyce had graduated from high school and had gone on to be a policewoman before she met Mbani. In comparison with the workers' wives and village women, she was well off. She was able to buy each new kanga that arrived and could afford sugar and other things when they were available.

When we had been in our new house for a few weeks, Joyce came down and announced, "Mama Beth, you must start wearing kangas. You shouldn't wear pants all the time!" (I had brought all my old pantsuits with me, thinking I'd wear them out and get a smashing new wardrobe on my return to Canada.) She took me to her house and gave me two of her kangas. Often I'd just wrap them over my jeans and the odd time over one of my cotton dresses. After a few months I was quite resigned to them – but the ironic thing was, I had given Joyce a pink pantsuit of mine which she wore with pride every time we went anywhere!

I might explain here that Tanzanian mothers are called by the name of their eldest son; if they have only girls, then by the name of their eldest girl. Hence Joyce was formally Mama Lkanga, Lkanga being her eldest son. They didn't know my other children, only Beth, so I was Mama Beth. Of course Joyce was always Joyce and I was Mama Betty when we talked privately, using the more formal title when in company.

By the time I was settled in at the ranch, I found I was picking up fragments of Swahili – not complete sentences, mind you, but enought to give the listener a fighting chance of understanding. Joyce could speak about the same amount of English, so our conversations were a mixture of the two languages, with a great deal of gesturing interspersed. We understood each other very well, but these conversations were the source of great merriment for any onlookers.

Sometimes we were able to buy bread in town, but often we couldn't, so I was forced to bake my own bread a good deal of the time. Each time I set a batch I'd make extra for Joyce, as she always shared with me. After a few loaves had changed hands, Joyce came one day and asked if I'd teach her to make bread. This was a little difficult – I didn't really use a recipe – but she'd sit and watch and jot it all down in Swahili on an old brown bag.

After watching a few times she decided she'd try a batch herself. The first time proved disastrous (even the chickens wouldn't eat it) but it wasn't long before she was coming down the hill, a lovely light loaf atop her head for me.

Whenever I ran out of propane and bread at the same time, I'd be forced to bake under rather primitive conditions. In Joyce's back kitchen was an ancient, heavy, cast-iron cook stove left by the Damms. It was the type our forefathers used, and it should have baked bread beautifully. However, the Africans I knew just didn't understand how the heat circulated around the oven, and Joyce was no exception. She filled the space where the hot air was to go with charcoal – absolutely packed it. For fuel she had to resort to great long chunks of trees which stuck out of the firebox as far as three feet, and Joyce would keep shoving it further in as it burned.

In any case, the smoke which belched forth from every crack and crevice was unbelievable. It fairly rolled around in the little room. We usually sat there while our bread was baking, as the loaves needed constant turning in order to cook evenly, so we'd crouch down low to keep under the billowing cloud of smoke. It was quite a sight. There were usually two or three other women with us and we'd visit away, coughing and sneezing and hiding our eyes.

By the time the bread was done and I was home once more, I'd smell like a burning barrel until I washed my hair and changed.

Yeast was very often unavailable, but luckily I had friends at home who kept me supplied. I had enough left over to give Joyce when it was in short supply, but I must admit the yeast I gave her was not used only to make bread. Joyce was very inventive and was always thinking up new ways to make a few shillings. She was one of the very best pombi brewers on the ranch, with a batch ready about every month to sell to the workers and the villagers who could afford it. If someone didn't have shillings she'd barter for some millet seed which she'd save for her next batch.

Pombi is a potent homebrew. It can be made of various

things, bananas and coconut being two of them, but millet seed is what was available and what Joyce used. She'd lay the millet seed out on my big patio, and there it would dry in the hot sun for a week or so. Of course children, goats and chickens would wander through it, leaving odd bits behind, but it didn't matter; the biggest glops would be lifted out and the rest would go in the boiling barrel with the millet. I don't remember how long Joyce boiled the mixture or what else she put in it – I do know she'd come for some yeast, thinking it would pack a better wallop. Not that it needed extra punch. Once a month every drinking man in the area would climb the hill to Joyce's house and sometime in the night would reel back down. I often thought it was a good thing the trail home was all downhill after a cup or two of Joyce's pombi.

Joyce was about seven months pregnant when we arrived at the ranch. Having had three children, she didn't anticipate any problems with her delivery, but she was concerned that the ranch Land Rover (the only vehicle available) would not be there when she went into labor. One day she came to me with a great thought. "Mama Betty, if the Land Rover is not here, then I want you to be my midwife." This she uttered as though she were asking for a loaf of bread. The mere thought just about blew my brains!

"Midwife? *Me?* I've never delivered a baby–"

"Mama, don't be silly. You had five children, and I saw your sewing shears. Yes, you are to be my midwife."

Well, I didn't mind using my sewing shears, but what bothered me was what I would need do with them!

The rest of that day and most of the night I stewed. I had helped deliver calves – but a baby! I'd never seen one born – even when I had my own, I kept my eyes glued shut till I had my lipstick back on. I knew the Land Rover was in town six nights out of seven and I also knew babies have a way of arriving in the wee small hours. Before morning I had my mind made up. I had to find out how to deliver a baby if, heaven forbid, I was forced to.

The very first chance I had, I visited the missionary doctor at the Moravian Mission some twelve miles out of Sumbawanga. His wife was a nurse as well as a midwife and I knew she delivered all the babies at their hospital. His eyes twinkled as I gasped out my tale of woe and his wife had the audacity to chortle out loud. I was invited to come and spend a few days. Bill was away as usual and Beth was in school, so out I went. It was the first of many visits and I always enjoyed my time spent there.

To make a long story short, after a few midnight experiences at the Mission I learned this age-old art and by the time I was to go back home I was delivering babies like a pro. But in the end my services weren't needed after all – Joyce was taken to the local government hospital, and I never had a chance to use my midwifery skills. What a shame!

Joyce, knowing how much I wanted to meet the people and get the real feel of the villagers, learn their culture and way of life, opened many doors I could never have approached. By this time she knew me well – I was an ignorant but harmless white lady who was not the least bit prejudiced. (Completely colorblind, Beth had told her.) Joyce made it possible for me to visit backwoods villages, events and celebrations I could not have seen otherwise. Only with a Tanzanian could I have enjoyed the wonderful opportunities that I did and that is but one reason I'll forever be grateful to Joyce.

On one of my trips to Mbeya to met Beth, who was enrolled in an international boarding school across the country, I asked Joyce to accompany me. I always stayed at least one night and many times two or three, and I would enjoy her chatterbox company. She was excited to say the least! The first thing she did was drag out all her clothes and rummage about to find what she thought was the classiest. We finally made it into town and got on the bus early in the morning. Now as I said before, Joyce was truly the uncrowned queen of Sumbawanga and area but still I thought I'd better check with her as to which hotel to stay in on arrival in Mbeya.

I usually stayed at the Mbeya Hotel, a railway hotel with a few comforts I really appreciated after being away for three months and roughing it in Sumbawanga. The staff, all Tanzanians, got to know me so well they treated me like royalty when I eventually arrived, all dusty and tired from the terrible bus trip. I've heard people say that the natives treat you well only for the bribes you give them. Well, in this instance it certainly wasn't so. Every time I arrived, even the cooks would come out to greet me. I know a lot of one-time-through tourists wondered what this odd white person did to merit such love and attention. I'm sure I don't know. I never gave them extra money or anything else. I think part of the reason might be I'd quiz them about their families, their work or whatever because I have this dreadful curiosity. But what I do know for sure is that everyone should have a "Mbeya hotel experience" at least once in a lifetime. It's truly balm to a dusty, troubled soul!

Joyce decided we should stay at a small, out-of-the-way guest house where she thought she'd be more comfortable, but even there she was very ill at ease – so much so, I thought, that in the future I would have to just enjoy her company at home and travel alone to meet Beth. But once we were back home, I found the trip hadn't been as daunting as I thought for Joyce. She came down next morning with a great smile: "Next time, let's go to Dar es Salaam!"

Joyce was extremely proud of the "bride price" Mbani had had to pay her father for her hand in marriage: six cows and forty goats, which I gathered was quite a lot. But then Joyce was not an ordinary village girl. She had taken as much schooling as she could obtain, about grade eleven, which in itself was amazing when 99 percent of the village girls were sold by their fathers at as young as twelve. Joyce then worked as a police officer until her marriage. The women of the area looked up to Joyce with good reason – she was an inspiration to many of them and helped them with their problems, materially and mentally.

Dr. Kilgour, I Presume?

After we were settled in – Beth was off to boarding school and Bill away for months at a time at the four ranches he was responsible for – I found time very heavy on my hands. I was truly bored to tears.

I decided to try to find something to do at the ranch to fill in the hours. I typed a little for the office – usually the letters they needed typed in English. The typist was trained but found English as hard to write as I did Swahili. Still I found the days long.

One day Mbani came in with a huge gash on his hand, wondering if I could bandage it for him. Could I! I've always had a private urge for nursing, lying dormant somewhere in my innards. If anyone within fifty miles had a sliver or a blister I'd practically beg them to let me at it! CUSO had given each of us a medical kit for ordinary, everyday first aid so I had a brainwave. As I bandaged away, I quizzed.

"Do you think I could run a little first aid centre here at the house for any medical mishaps that might arise?"

"Well," he answered, glancing at the sloppy bandage on his hand, "with a bit of practice I believe you could be a help to us!"

I was in business! The clinic (to use the term very loosely) was a success – possibly not in the medical sense but certainly in public relations. The CUSO officers in Dar es Salaam kept me in basic medical kits and if I needed some other item like boracic acid or peroxide they would shop about and find it for me.

It became commonplace to come down in the morning to find ten or twelve village mamas waiting on my patio for me and my medical expertise!

Of course, a lot of times they used it for an excuse to pop in for a cup of tea, which I served every afflicted person who happened by. Bill accused me of running out to the road looking for patients, but that wasn't so. Maybe to the end of the walk!

43

Many times the ailment proved to be a ten-year-old scar which would be pointed to with great solemnity and much sadness in the vocal cords. In cases like this I'd just get out my hydrogen peroxide and dab some on. They'd see it bubble up and be very impressed. This never failed to reward me with great respect – it must be powerful medicine to bubble so! Prosper as a rule stayed close by in case my Swahili – or lack of it – got me in trouble, and also to keep the teapot going.

There were many humorous situations during my two years of clinicing, some due to my lack of experience and others due to misunderstandings.

One time a twelve-year-old girl from a very backwoods village had been hoeing with her *jembe* in the maize patch. The jembe is a heavy hunk of steel stuck on the end of a short handle, sort of resembling our garden hoe. It's very awkward and with the ground so hard you can belt yourself a terrible blow. Many a foot has been chopped with this instrument and that's exactly what happened to this girl. She gave a vicious dig, sliced her bare foot and the mechanic's sons brought her to me, scared stiff and bleeding all the way. She was not the least bit eager to put her bleeding foot in my care, but with the boys' help we got her sitting down with the foot in antiseptic and water. Meanwhile I got out the supplies I thought I needed – with many gasps of fright from her, I might add. She reminded me of a trapped animal, so I smiled a lot and patted her back.

Finally I reached for my gigantic sewing shears to cut the bandage and this was the last straw. The poor girl thought I was going to chop her toe right off, and bolted to the door like the very devil was behind her. Prosper ran after her and explained in the tribal language that I didn't chop pieces and boil them up, and I really was a kind soul – even though a strange color.

The western world is not the only place that harbors hypochondriacs, and we had our share of them. One man especially, Jumamosi, nearly drove me crazy. You've heard of "my man, Friday?" Well, *Jumamosi* means Saturday in Swahili so I guess he was my man Saturday – only I didn't want him for my man! He was on my doorstep four or five times a week, with a headache, stomachache, sore knee – whatever he could invent.

I'd usually give him a Sucaryl pill or an aspirin or even orange Kool-aid with halibut liver oil in it – anything I thought might relieve his mind, where most of his troubles were. During the last week of our term I was out of almost everything, but Jumamosi showed up with a long face. "I have a terrible sore here, Mama," as he pointed to his tongue. I looked closely and could see nothing, no redness or sores, so I reached in my drawer, grabbed a tube and applied some ointment. He shuddered, smiled happily and off he went. After he left, it occurred to me to check the label on the tube. It was athlete's foot ointment!

All my encounters with patients were not funny ones, or just with lonely or curious people. I treated a lot of bad gashes, some just to stop the bleeding until we could get them to town for stitches. But the cases which never failed to break my heart were the little burn victims. In the villages and the workers' homes the mothers cook outside. They lay a circle of stones and set the fire in the centre. Then they place a screen of sorts or a flat stone in the fire to set their cooking pots on. The little children, especially the toddlers or those crawling, were the most vulnerable. They would be playing about and trip or fall into the fire, and the burns they received were dreadful. The worst one I saw, or at least the one which remains in my memory, was about eight months after I started the clinic.

The child was just a year old, and it was after dark when the poor mother came to my door. He was in shock, had a terrible burn under his chin and on his neck where he had landed on the fire, and one arm was blistered from contact with the hot rocks.

The poor mother was desperate and so was I! I was sure the child would die so I wrapped him in a sheet, handed him to the mother and ran out to see if the Land Rover was home. Of course it wasn't and there was no other way to get the child to the hospital. I knew he didn't stand a chance unless I could help. I wrapped him up warmly, crushed some aspirin in juice with a tiny sip of brandy and held him for an hour. After he responded a bit I cleaned the burns as well as I could, sprinkled sulpha powder in them and very loosely bandaged the open neck wounds. I knew you should never bandage burns, but if I didn't infection was sure to set in, knowing village life as I did.

Anyway, the mama took him home and for a week she'd bring him up in the morning and I'd walk down to her village in the late afternoon, changing and cleaning the burns. (You cannot leave medicine with natives to administer every four hours or whatever. They feel, "Well, if a little helps, I'll take it all and be better immediately!")

The baby recovered and when we were leaving, the mother came to say goodbye and brought the baby, now a two-year-old. I looked closely and there wasn't a scar to behold. Pure luck on my part – and a *very* long prayer!

For any patient with an eye infection, which included nearly all the children, I would have to administer the antibiotics myself. I spent a great deal of time walking up and down Melenji hill! At times I ran out of antibiotic eyedrops, so I had the office send me good old-fashioned boracic acid which, if I never missed a wash, worked wonderfully well.

The government hospital in town was really dreadful. I love the Tanzanians and I love the country but I cannot accept those awful hospitals! They are dirty beyond belief; the old bandages and casts are tossed out the windows to collect flies. The boiling of the instruments is done in huge black earthenware bowls outside over an open fire. The sheets are changed so seldom, they smell, and I'll never forget visiting Joyce when she was in labor and being horrified – as only sheltered and overindulged people can be. I came home and told Bill, "No matter what happens, don't *ever* put me in that place. I'd rather lie in a ditch than go to that place!" Then guess what? I broke my ankle and wound up there!

I had been taking Beth back to school and the bus got into Sumbawanga very late one night. Bill was home at the time and was there to meet me. I had to go to the bathroom in the worst way, so I went across the street. There are no street lights in Sumbawanga and it was very dark. I went up some steps and along to the bar where I thought the restroom was, but found it was the wrong one. I came out and went along to the next one but between the two buildings was a four-foot drop I didn't know about and couldn't see! Boy, did I go down, my ankle twisted under me. Bill carried me to the Land Rover and home.

Next day I went to the hospital for an X-ray. Broken ankle. I got a cast – the old plaster-of-Paris kind – and although it was my ankle that was broken, the cast went halfway up my thigh! It weighed more than I did. Anyway, when I woke up after the setting, there I was in that very hospital – dirty sheets and all! I was supposed to stay overnight because they were afraid of shock. I didn't tell them *my* shock was waking up there!

At home, with crutches and a lot of practice, I managed. Coming down the bedroom steps was the worst till I found that if I sat down and shinneyed down on my bottom, it worked great – rather like those machines that wear off flab with moving belts!

In all fairness, there were several mission hospitals in the area that were a completely different story. But to get to them you needed a vehicle, and that is the downfall of Tanzania. Vehicles are few, the roads are terrible and you can't get to help when you need it.

The mission I loved to visit was the Moravian mission, Kilingala. It was started by a little Danish woman and while we were there was run by a Swedish doctor and his wife. Third in command was a Tanzanian doctor, Joseph Sipemba, who was educated in Denmark and is now in charge of the mission.

There was also a Dutch schoolteacher there to teach Dr. Harry's two children. Dr. Harry and his wife and family were due to go home in a year and they needed to teach the children once more how to behave like Swedes! They could speak Swahili fluently, but were forgetting their Swedish schooling.

The hospital at Kilingala was certainly a Third World hospital, sparse in our eyes but it was absolutely spotless and had more money to buy supplies than did the government hospitals. The nurses were trained by Dr. Harry's wife and were capable and clean.

Dr. Harry even learned to work with one witch doctor for the good of the people. The witch doctor would often refer patients to Harry and if one had a psychosomatic illness, the witch doctor would be called in. One gentleman thought he had a snake spirit in his stomach, and he was sure it would eat him inside out. Though he had no physical ailment, he was very troubled. So Dr.

Harry and the witch doctor hatched an idea.

Harry, the witch doctor and the patient sat around a table near an open window. Harry put a big spike on the table and told the patient that the snake would come out of his body when the witch doctor called it, and its spirit would go into the spike instead. Meanwhile the witch doctor was holding a magnet under the table. He gave a few chants and, lo and behold, the spike slithered! Harry seized it and threw it with a great flourish out the window. The man was cured on the spot, and happiness reigned near Kilingala!

The Catholic mission in town had three or four nursing sisters who ran the immunization program the government had brought in. All children, villagers or not, had to be immunized and the sisters not only gave the shots but also tried to teach the village mamas the basics of cleanliness and good nutrition. I remember one of the nurses saying,"Why do I try? They promise they will follow my program and then go home and do everything like it's been done for centuries!" Which is understandable. If someone came and tried to change me overnight I'd be a bit upset! I think the way to go is to try and keep the young girls in school and teach them the healthier way – through the young the changes will come.

One of the German sisters was a dentist and quite a good one, although half the time she didn't have freezing compound. Most Tanzanians didn't mind but I had to have a filling and although she never hurt me, I was sure hanging onto the chair!

One big difference I found was in the attitudes of the missionaries, whether they were teachers or nurses or doctors – so different from the churches here at home who feel God is only in their particular camp! They all helped the natives' bodies first and foremost and *then* came the saving of souls. These fine people, whether they were Catholic or Protestant, were good friends and worked together for the common good of all. The Catholic priests would run off all their brochures on the Moravian printing press, and if a new mission opened, all were invited. That impressed me.

Carl and Rigmor were Danish missionaries who lived in

town, but worked in the whole area. Carl was a carpenter among other things, and Rigmor, who was a nurse, worked with the women in the villages. I spent many happy hours in their company, helping where I could with sewing.

Carlos and Joanne Moyer and their three children were in charge of a mission near the Zambian border. Joanne's father had been in charge of it years before – in fact, Joanne was born there. She went on to take her R.N. and married Carlos, who had taken his Bible training at Prairie Bible Institute at Three Hills, Alberta, which just again proves what a small world we live in as Three Hills is where we live.

Carlos, with no actual training in the medical field, read every textbook he could lay his hands on and became very capable, treating everything and operating, even on eyes. There are many natives in the area who have their eyesight intact thanks to Carlos' healing hands.

Creatures Great and Small

When 99 percent of the world's population thinks about Africa, their thoughts soon turn to snakes and other creepy-crawlies.

At our headquarters near Sumbawanga there were very few creatures – for the simple reason that the people were so hungry, anything that moved was eaten. There were times the villagers would burn off the prairie grass so that they could dig the ground rats from their holes to eat. (The ranch butchered twice a week, but this meat was taken to town for sale and the villagers would get just the stomach or intestines for a few shillings, or nothing at all if they had no money.)

The one pest I tangled with once or twice was the army ant. If you get in their way, you are covered in a moment and they are nearly impossible to kill.

There were puff adders on the ranch – I saw the holes each time I walked up to Joyce's. But I never saw a live snake on that ranch. Children played all day in the grass, but I suppose they made so much noise that the snakes got out of the way. The odd cow would be bitten, possibly because they were herding so close together the snake was trapped, and once in a while one of the men would kill a snake. It was always brought to Bill if he was home. He gave them twenty shillings for it and he'd skin it. The natives will not touch a snake, even a dead one. They figure the whole snake is poisonous and they're taking no chances. It absolutely horrified the onlookers when Beth wrapped a dead one around her neck – of course, it did nothing for my stomach either!

There were a few monkeys near the ranch. In fact, there was a man hired just to stay in the maize field and keep the monkeys out.

I saw black millipedes and stick spiders, especially near the start of the wet season. That was when the insects really came out. The stick spiders are strange creatures. They look a lot like our daddy-longlegs but have longer legs and, I thought, a skinnier body. And then what house would be complete without the little geckos, the funny little lizards that crawl on the walls and ceilings in tropical countries; they are really fascinating and they keep down the flies and other bugs. The odd time, one of them would discover how cosy it was amidst the bedclothes. So before Beth would come home I'd shake everything up good and change the sheets, but once in a while she'd still find somebody sleeping in her bed. If I heard her shriek like a banshee, I knew I'd have to tear up the steps with my broom and bat the poor gecko until it either ran away or died of ruptured eardrums.

There were many chameleons in the Sumbawanga area. I saw them on the ranch several times. If I didn't disturb them they remained a lovely bright, lime-green color, but if I tried to move them they quickly turned a mud color which blended in with the grasses to perfection.

There were beautiful hummingbirds which stayed close to some of my flowers, and little yellow finches, but not much else in the bird department. Of course while travelling I saw many more – the ugliest was the Malibu stork, which didn't merit its glamorous name.

Once in a while, someone would accidentally get between a hippo and his pool and would suffer a terrible bite, but there were not too many of these mishaps.

At one point, Bill was forced to shoot a baboon which was causing great damage in the manager's maize *shamba* (garden). Bill said it was almost like shooting a human being and he hoped he would never have to do that again.

One real pest at Uvinza ranch was the tsetse fly. These are flat ugly flies, larger than our houseflies, and they pack a terrible bite. Bill had a little Honda motorbike for getting around on the ranch which was very scattered. He found he had to go twenty-five miles an hour to beat the tsetse fly, which would bite right through his denim shirt.

The cattle at all the ranches are driven into a dip and forced to swim it twice a week to protect them from tics and tsetse flies and the diseases they cause – sleeping sickness and East Coast Fever. Wild animals are immune to these diseases but are carriers.

Uvinza Ranch

Bill, Beth and I were fortunate indeed that one of the four ranches Bill had to look after was the wonderful Uvinza ranch. This ranch, in Bill's own words, was heaven on earth! Personally I wouldn't go that far, but it was great.

The ranch was big, over a hundred and fifty thousand acres, with marvelous producing capacity. At that time, they were busy relocating the headquarters to a more central position, so new roads, as well as all the offices and other buildings, had to be built.

Bill spent two thirds of his term either at Uvinza or travelling to and from. I loved to visit this place, partly because it was like slipping into Africa of old. Whenever Beth was at school and I could leave my clinic for a few days, I'd try to catch a ride there.

It took two ordinary days of travel, stopping overnight in the dusty little town of Mpanda. The trip was rough, as only African travel can be, but it was worth it. The scenery was magnificent and I'd always see animals – not in a reserve, but roaming wild. On one trip we ran upon a family unit of giraffes – to me the most beautiful of animals – right on the road. We had ample opportunity to enjoy them before they swept away. In some areas where giraffes are prevalent, the telephone lines have to be raised six feet higher. The male can stand seventeen feet tall.

We often saw cats – wild ones but very like our pet housecats – and families of mongooses. Monkeys of all descriptions would dash across the road, with the mothers tearing back after their dawdling infants. One day we were on our way into the little town of Uvinza and saw a zebra, two snakes, mongooses and a crocodile.

Every few miles the scenery would change completely, from vast open plains to areas with huge boulders, often with a lion warming himself in the late sun. There were trees of all varieties and flowers by the million – all the glory only Africa could produce.

The main attraction in the little town of Uvinza was a club at the salt mine. This club was usually full of men, with just the odd waitress and some prostitutes about. All that really went on there was drinking, with a dance once in a while. At the doors, local ladies would set up a fire and cook goat meat which they'd sell, garnished with chili peppers. The meat was usually tough as an old tire but if chewed well with the hot chilis it was fine.

The world is a very small place, I found, the first time I visited the club. There on the windows were curtains made of the very same fabric – color, pattern, everything – as the material I had made into hot pants for one of my daughters a couple of years before I left Canada.

The trailer Bill lived in at Uvinza ranch was small. *Really* small. I've seen bigger doll houses. It boasted a fold-down table, a plank cupboard, and two built-in seats with storage space underneath. The bed was also built in, a plank with a chunk of foam for a mattress. No sane person could stand that trailer for more than twenty minutes. All the cooking was done on a Chinese kerosene hot plate, one burner with a round of wicks circling it. If you planned, say, meat, potatoes and one vegetable, you'd have to start at nine in the morning to get it all cooked and then reheated for the meal. It took some practice, let me tell you.

The drinking water came from the Malagrasi River, not far from the trailer. The boys would take a tank down, fill it up, haul it back and dump it in the old barrel at the corner. This river supported crocodiles, hippos and I don't know how many villages upstream, so the water needed boiling and filtering. All I ever got from it was a bad case of hives!

At night we were lulled to sleep by the lions roaring and the hippos grunting, each within yards of the trailer. All the cattle were brought in each night by the herder and locked in bomas constructed of twelve-foot-high thornbush and supposedly lion-proof. The thorns were a good four inches long and the construction should have kept the predators out, but every month or so a lion would leap over it, grab a cow in his jaws and leap back out. I'd better add here that African cattle, at least the ones I saw, were much smaller than Alberta ones! In this region too, you could see the real Ankola cattle, the same breed as that depicted on tombs and walls in ancient Egypt.

I couldn't believe how big the lions really were. One day a lioness which had been shot had to be loaded in the Land Rover and I went along. It was not a large one, I was told, but I swear her paws would fill a dinner plate, and the front teeth were inches long. It took five people to load her into the truck. Another amazing fact was that the night watchman shot the lions with a shotgun, using slugs. Many times the ranch manager, Mr. Hingi, would give him only one slug! Talk about living dangerously!

When the first families moved up to the new headquarters they were forced to keep fires blazing all night as they still lived in thatched huts and the lions were such a threat.

The people themselves would go into their huts at sunset and bar the doors until morning, but Bill and I would spray the trailer for mosquitoes and close it up and go for a walk each evening. We often heard rustling in the bushes and the odd grunt but we never saw a thing. Whether we were foolish or not I'll never know, but we just were not afraid.

There was quite a bit of poaching done for ivory, which was sad. Bill had seen a lame cow elephant with a calf. She had been caught in a snare and managed to break free, but she was weak and still had a chunk of the wire around her leg. The natives seemed much more afraid of the elephants than of the lions. Elephants, they said, could trample you and your house, and wreck your shambas. They destroy everything, but a lion is cowardly!

One evening Bill was reading on the bed and I went out to the *choo* (outdoor toilet) before retiring. It was just a little tin shelter with a wobbly door on it, hanging open. I reached the door and lifted my foot to step in but for some unknown reason, happened to glance down. There, right below my raised foot, was a shiny black snake. That glance saved my life. I just stood still and the snake slid off down a hole. I wasn't even upset. When I got back to the trailer I told Bill I had seen this lovely black snake and all he did was grunt and turn a page. The next morning I told the ranch manager about it and he turned pale –

well, as pale as an African can.

"If that snake had struck you, you would have been dead in five minutes!" he exclaimed. "But of course, we have the stone!" The "stone" was a special little rock you laid on a snake bite and it was supposed to draw out the snake venom. I wasn't impressed! The rock was kept in the office safe, and half the time the keys to the office would be missing!

I had another animal experience at the Uvinza ranch. One evening Bill was laid up with a touch of malaria and we had run out of coffee so I told him I'd walk up to Hingi's and borrow a little, replacing it the next day when we were going into town. It was a lovely warm, dark night. I walked along with my forever-dull flashlight, got the coffee from Debbie, had a short chat and started for home. Halfway back I heard a strange rustling noise by the side of the trail. I shone my flashlight very warily and planned my next move: run like holy old H. The beam shone on a porcupine. A big one! Now I can hear all and sundry laughing, but let me tell you, the African porcupine is a lot bigger than our little squatty ones. Its quills are a good ten inches long – the needles on this one stood higher than my waist, and I'm five-four and short-waisted! But it just moved away as I stood there marvelling at it. I was to stand quietly a great many times while in Africa!

At this ranch they butchered only once a month, and the people were so poor, they couldn't even buy the scrapings. It's little wonder they were so grateful for the game Bill could kill with his .243 Winchester. Some game animals were too big for it, but the plains abound with all sizes of antelope, right down to the tiny, dainty dik-diks. Bill was in his glory. He could hunt all day, fill his Land Rover and every scrap of meat was gone by morning. The people were so hungry that Bill had permission to feed them – for the betterment of the ranch, he was told.

Each hunting safari he'd take four or five guys with him, at least one of them Muslim, so when he shot something they could jump out, slit its throat and turn it towards Mecca while saying a prayer. (They would never eat wart hog as it was pork and thus unclean.) Bill would come back with the Land Rover, dropping off game here and there at homes, and the natives would be delighted.

Sometimes Bill was too busy to go out so I'd be delegated to get the meat. I've always enjoyed hunting – not just for the kill but for the adventure. I mostly went after wart hog. It's delicious meat – just like pork, only with the fat rippling throughout the meat instead of encircling it. I found the wart hog easy to hunt and lots of fun. Now before any armchair conservationists get inflamed about this, let me explain. These people – including us many times – were hungry. There was little food in the area and the children had the distended bellies and dull eyes indicative of poor nutrition. These are the ones who ate my wart hogs and I just wish I could have shot more for them. I would shoot two or three whenever I could get the gun and the Land Rover at the same time.

I always had a group of Tanzanian boys to help me spot game, and how they enjoyed it. Just like a circus – going out on safari with a strange white mama with yellow pants and blue eyes! A woman with a gun!

I remember one expedition in particular. Wart hogs can be dangerous if cornered; they do have tusks and can slash an unwary visitor very quickly and easily. We were driving along a roadway in the middle of the *pori* (plain), and I was in the back with the boys watching for signs. All of a sudden someone shouted, "There's one, Mama Beth!" It wasn't too big – in fact, I thought it would make good tender chops. The little .243 should take care of it nicely. I aimed carefully, squeezing off gently like Bill, the master, had taught me. Down it went and all the boys piled over the sides, I only slightly more sedately. But just as I got near it, up it got with a great grunt, revenge in its beady eyes. (Not that I blamed it. I'd hate someone who shot at me!)

I hastily popped another bullet in the chamber and shot once more. I turned to tell the boys all was well and there wasn't a soul in sight! They had all bolted when the animal got up and they weren't hanging around – if I did, that was my business! After a couple of shouts they all came back, two or three at a time, looking sheepish. It's a good thing I hadn't needed a backup – I'd have been out of luck. But I can't blame them. A wounded wart hog is nothing to fool with.

One thing that amazed the men was the fact that I shot left-handed. For a very good reason – I *am* left-handed – but they thought I was so good right-handed, I was deliberately handicapping myself!

It was at Uvinza that Bill had quite an experience one day. It was dark and raining very hard. He had been to town and was on his way back to the ranch in the Land Rover. A little old native stopped him and asked for a ride. He said he had been walking home and had to stop quickly when he noticed a pride of lions lying on the road.

"I picked up some stones to throw at them," he said as he showed Bill a few pebbles. "Then I backed away and ran, *bwana!*"

Bill had others in the front, so he told the man to climb in the back. He drove along and as he glanced up, he noticed two bright green lights in an overhanging tree. One passenger said, "It's *chui*," meaning leopard. The poor native in the back just hit the deck. But his day wasn't over. Bill was barreling along at a good clip and directly in front of him on the road was a great blob. By the time he got the Land Rover stopped, slipping and sliding, he realized what he had just about accomplished. Directly in front of him was the hind end of an elephant and he had come very close to driving under it! All the while the poor native was hanging on for dear life in the back. The elephant stepped off into the ditch and trumpeted right in his ear!

What a day that fellow had had. I imagine he'll be telling kith and kin fireside tales for years to come.

The Uvinza ranch was in the backwoods and most of the natives in the area had never seen a white woman. When I showed up the first time, you can imagine the stir I caused. When the workers saw me they ran to their huts to get the wives and children to come and view this strange apparition. I was wearing a bright yellow pantsuit and awful sunglasses (I have such trouble getting a fit on my pug nose – these had purple frames) and with strange hair and skin, it was as though a walking circus act had arrived.

Some kids were brave enough to pinch my skin and giggle

but others howled and ran and hid behind their mothers. Bill, watching closely, noted the look of instant flight in my eyes and sternly told me to stand still. "They've never seen anything like *you* before!"

It was near Uvinza where Stanley met Livingstone and there's a granite monument at the spot. Along the same path are mango trees which are not indigenous but were planted by the Arabs to mark the slave route to the sea – a really tragic memorial, and one I have vividly remembered.

Also near Uvinza, we saw homemade bikes made entirely of wood, seat and all. The people would push them up the hills, climb on and ride down. The handlebars wouldn't steer; this was accomplished by leaning whichever way you wanted to turn. To negotiate a real turn, you had to get off and pull the whole affair around. These bicycles were used mostly to carry firewood, which was tied together in a bundle behind the seat.

Witchcraft

I'm sure most of us in the West would have trouble putting much faith in witchcraft. But whether we believe in it or not, witchcraft plays an intricate part in many, many lives in Africa even today.

If you simply go the tourist route in Africa for a month or two, you might never notice the power it wields. There are huge Christian churches in all centres, large and small. There are little mud churches in most villages that I visited, but still the witch doctor plays a powerful role in the lives of even the well-educated Africans.

As I have mentioned, Joyce was pregnant when we arrived at the ranch, with the baby due in June. She waited, and waited – July and still no baby. Soon it was August and she was terribly uncomfortable. She went to the doctor at the government hospital in Sumbawanga. These doctors are trained but most do not have their diplomas because it takes money to take the tests. He checked her over and figured she had miscalculated. He told her to wait another week.

By the end of that week she was really miserable, so on the way home she visited a witch doctor in Essessa village. He, for a fee, told her two women, one in town and one on the ranch, wanted her dead and had put a curse on her. "They are jealous of your position," he said. Joyce was convinced the one in town was Sophia, Mbani's mistress of the moment. He gave Joyce some powder to take to remove the curse and told her the baby would arrive in three days' time. She came home and told me the story. Nothing happened, and by now Joyce's ankles were swelling.

After five days she went back to the government doctor, who admitted her to the hospital and induced labor. She had painful contractions for three days, but that was all, and Joyce began to slip away. The doctor finally performed a Caesarian. Joyce survived, but the baby did not. I couldn't help but wish she had gone to a mission hospital where they could have saved the baby.

The saddest thing was that when Joyce finally came home,

she was sure for months that it was the curse that had caused her trouble and that it indeed was still on her. I tried to console her in my Western way, but all she said was, "You don't understand, Mama Beth. I will still die soon!"

Sumbawanga region was, at one time, a real haven for witch doctors. There were literally thousands of them. But the year before we arrived, the government stepped in and removed them to the far reaches of the country, splitting them up. By the time we left they were slowly drifting back.

The natives are very superstitious in the first place and the witch doctors thrive on this. One problem I had at my house was thieving – nothing too big, just little things that were important to me. When we arrived we had two clocks, but it wasn't long until all I had left to tell the time was an old pocketwatch of Bill's. This I hung on a nail in a place I thought not a soul would notice, but no such luck. One morning it was gone. Well, the fat hit the fire and I went to Mbani with my tale of woe, padding it copiously with tears. All he said was there wasn't a thing he could do! But he was bright – he had had an idea all along, which he couldn't tell me in case I blabbed.

He went to one witch doctor in the village he figured the watch was in, and they came up with a plan. The witch doctor called his people about and told them to watch. He threw some kind of dust in his open fire, voiced a few incantations and then told his audience that the fire would show the thief's face the next day. Word spread, and lo and behold, when Prosper came to work next morning he found the watch on our doorstep!

The natives, to me, seemed unafraid of the police although the police could be very cruel. They are, however, very afraid of the witch doctor. He really holds their very spirit in his hands and can manipulate them very easily into believing just about anything.

Joyce was devastated when her husband Mbani took Sophia, his favorite mistress at the time, as his second wife. She came to me in tears, saying she was leaving and could I give her two thousand shillings to put a down payment on a little house in Kongwa. I gave it to her and several months later, when I asked if she had got a house, she told me she had used the money to go to a special witch doctor. She had asked him to put a hex on Sophia so Mbani would not go near her. The witch doctor took her money, gave her some powder to sprinkle over Sophia's doorstep and told her Mbani would never cross Sophia's step again if she followed his orders. She did, but of course Mbani continued going to Sophia's place and Joyce lost the money.

Another time, one of the ranch workers was visiting at another village and he slept with one of the wives of a chief. The chief found out and had his particular witch doctor cast a spell on the worker. Lightning was to strike and kill him the following Wednesday. Joyce and her family were present when the argument took place and she was very distraught. "George is going to be killed, Mama Beth, on Wednesday!" I tried to calm her and told her nothing would happen. All she said was, "You don't understand, Mama."

When the dreaded Wednesday had come and gone I brought it up again, but she just shook her head. "It'll still happen!"

I could understand the village natives believing so completely in witchcraft, but many educated natives have great difficulty ignoring it.

In the town of Sumbawanga a young Tanzanian, an ordained Moravian minister, was the head clergyman of the big church in town. Each Sunday he'd hold two services and preach a real old-fashioned hellfire-and-brimstone sermon. But during the week, if he had problems with his family or someone else, off he'd go to the witch doctor!

What was really sad was that an innocent person could be branded a witch and be so completely shunned by all those around her, it was as if she didn't exist. A wife of one of the main ranch workers had this problem while I was there. It had started so simply. Someone had eaten at her hut and was very sick to his stomach that night. It wasn't long before it was all over the ranch that she had cast a spell on him and was a powerful witch. Everyone completely ignored her, afraid she would cast a wicked spell on them.

She was a hard-working lady, not cheerful but basically good. She had had ten children, four of whom had died at various ages and this still affected her. I felt so sorry for her. She'd sneak over to my house with her kanga draped over her head and just sit and sip tea, and then slide away again into the shadows. Of course after a few months, this was all forgotten as something else happened of interest.

I often thought, "What if someone gets the notion I'm a witch?" It certainly could happen. I was the odd man out at the ranch and the only white person for miles. I asked Joyce about this one day and she gave a great belly laugh. "No, no, Mama Beth. We know you have no power. We know you're harmless!"

I was much relieved!

It seemed very easy to blame others for any sad or unexpected event. One day, the ten-year-old son of one of the workers was playing out in the trees. He took very ill and died within a few hours. Someone decided Norman, the tractor driver, had poisoned the child because he had been rude to him and Norman had given him the dickens. The doctor in town told me later that the children had been playing with poisonous leaves and the boy had eaten one on a dare. But it was months before Norman was accepted back into the little group.

Joyce and I went to the boy's funeral, and that day will haunt my memory forever. First we went to a little house in town belonging to a relative. The poor mother, surrounded by relatives, was huddled on the floor behind the open coffin, which was just a hastily-put-together plank affair. The whole of the little house was full of crouching natives wailing and moaning. After about two hours of this the undertaker arrived and, with a hammer and great spikes, nailed the lid in front of the mother. The coffin was taken to the big Moravian church where the minister said prayers, and then by Land Rover to the graveyard, which was just a gigantic weed patch with the odd wooden stake to mark the graves. As the coffin was lowered the mother fell in on top of it, wailing and weeping, and the men had to pull her out.

The ritual took all day, and what bothered me the most was that I could not do one thing to help the mother. I think our funerals are barbaric here at home at times, but there is usually a bit of comfort to be gained from them. This was straight pain from beginning to end.

One thing I did learn while in Africa was that there are many, many things happening in the native villages that our Western minds could never comprehend.

Oh, My Aching Bones!

Travel in Tanzania is strictly for the hardy of heart. We're so spoiled in the Western world with hardtop and good gravel, not to mention well-maintained vehicles, that we found it very hard to get used to travel in Tanzania.

The roads, all except a few, are quite dreadful. Most reminded me of the old-time cattle trails used in pioneer times in the west. The people have real problems trying to keep the roads even usable, partly because of lack of funds and partly because of the weather. During the dry season a person can usually get through, although you'll be dusty and saddlesore on arrival! But when the rains come they can be terrible. One thing I learned very quickly: always allow yourself an extra couple of days to get to your destination. You could sail through (sort of) or you could have all sorts of delays.

Beth was enrolled in a school at Moshi; she would attend for three months and then have a month's furlough. When holiday time arrived she'd catch the night bus down to Dar es Salaam (which was okay – it was hardtop) and then the train to Mbeya which also was fine. (The Chinese had built this railway and it was well-maintained, and some of the Chinese were still there to see that it ran on time.) Then I would take the bus from Sumbawanga and meet her in Mbeya. There we'd spend two or three days relaxing and shopping. We'd then catch the bus back home and this was the hard part of the trip.

The buses were very old and decrepit and, when combined with the awful roads, they guaranteed that you never knew when you'd arrive or in what shape. The trip was only about two hundred miles but boy, they were tough miles! I'd leave Sumbawanga at seven in the morning, and just getting on the bus was an adventure.

They sell the tickets right on the bus and there always seemed to be four times as many prospective passengers as tickets. Standing in line was something the natives couldn't handle gracefully. You would have to see the shoving and elbowing that went on. Not gentle little tugs or pushes. I mean out-and-out war. One time I was attempting to get on the bus in Sumbawanga and I was knocked right off my feet. Norman, the tractor driver, was across the street and ran in like a little bantam rooster and pushed and shoved until he saw me safely stowed aboard. I think it was then that I too learned to shove and poke with the best of them. One time I was just putting my foot on the bottom step and a great six-foot-four Tanzanian came down on top of it. Before I realized it, I had landed a real left hook on his ear and another on his neck!

Then, when you get on the bus, you head for a seat. The only difference between first class and ordinary seats is the lack of chickens and goats. It was fun travelling, though. Time didn't matter and everyone aboard was happy and cheerful. The odd time a goat would get loose but it didn't matter – we were so packed in, it couldn't go far. Usually at the high hills all passengers would get out and walk, with the empty bus trundling up behind, wheezing away. Bill was on one once that was so out of shape, the men passengers had to pull it up with a stout chain!

There were usually two or three stops enroute and kids would come around selling roasted groundnuts and bananas. Usually we'd pack a bit of lunch to take and a thermos with orange juice – sometimes with *konyagi* in it! It seemed to dull the aches and pains.

We'd get into Mbeya anytime from ten at night until two or three, or sometimes not till next morning. The taxi drivers got to know us, we travelled the route so often. "How are things in Sumbawanga, Mama?" they'd ask. Of course I was the odd one – the Mama from Sumbawanga.

During one period, there was a lot of smuggling going on, and the bus would be stopped and searched by soldiers carrying guns. This happened so often the soldiers got to know me, and would come up with a great grin and handshake.

The trip home would be a repeat and then a month later, back we'd go for Beth's classes once more.

The odd time I'd go all the way, first by bus, then by train to Dar or to meet Bill for a CUSO meeting and our shots. Dar was extremely hot and humid and one could wear only very loose light cottons and thongs. Beth and I would shop for two hours and head back to our hotel where we'd be forced to shower and cool off before attempting it again.

The shops in Dar were funny little ones, each of them unique. Our favorites were the Indian shops where silk was sold for the saris. It was all so beautiful, it would take your breath away. There was also a real old ice cream parlor in Dar that we always headed for. The ice cream, although not as rich as ours at home, was manna from heaven in our eyes – or taste buds! You learned to appreciate even very little things like an ice cream cone when stationed away. There was a bookstore where I managed to buy Shakespeare's complete works for Beth – for about three dollars.

There were several movie houses which showed mostly Chinese films. These were rather inferior but really hilarious with lots of Kung Fu and dragons. The audiences used to get right in the action with lots of cheering and laughing going on throughout.

One thing I noticed about Dar – the doors and windows were locked and barred all the time, and the motorbikes had two or three hefty chains wound round and through them with great padlocks holding them. I guess there was a lot of thievery in the city – not unlike our big cities, I suppose. One CUSO volunteer in Dar had had his radio stolen many times. Finally, in desperation, he padlocked it to his bed – only to come home and find that the headboard, radio and all, had vanished!

We'd stock up on everything we could in Dar and head home. It was always nice to get back to the ranch and the peaceful lifestyle we enjoyed there.

The roads were dreadfully hard on vehicles. Bill had a new Land Rover to use for travelling from ranch to ranch, but in one year's time it was a complete write-off – just a pile of junk.

If something went wrong with a tractor or wagon, the problem would wait months and sometimes years before being fixed. No one ever got too excited – nothing was really kept in what we would call top condition. "Maybe tomorrow" was the motto.

Comrades and Characters

Many real characters came our way while we were posted in Tanzania – too many to mention them all here, but I'll tell of a few.

One was a fellow called Rutiewa. He was the assistant veterinarian at the ranch when we arrived; whether he had training in this field or not, I never found out. Rutiewa was a troublemaker with a very loud mouth, more so when full of pombi which was half the time.

One night Bill just happened to be home and we were fast asleep upstairs when we were awakened by someone shouting "Kilga!" (They could never get their tongues around our last name!) He jumped up, thinking the cattle, which had been brought in for slaughter next morning, had broken out. He ran out but was back very quickly with orders.

"Don't open this door for anyone but me, Bets. Lock it securely!"

My curiosity, always on the alert, really leaped. The night was black but I could hear all sorts of shouting. Soon I heard the Land Rover take off down the hill. About fifteen minutes later it was back, with even more shouting going on. By the time Bill returned to the house, I was just about a basket case.

What had happened, in a nutshell, was that Rutiewa had gotten drunk, taken his *panga* and tried to kill Mbani the manager. He sliced the back of his head a terrible blow, which if half an inch higher, the doctor said, would have been fatal. They rushed him to the doctor and brought the police back to hunt for the culprit who had run away.

They found him in his hut, covered with blood, sure he had killed Mbani and hoping so out of jealousy. He was quite resigned to going along to jail. He was lucky, though. He was brought before a judge who belonged to the same tribe as himself and was given only two years. And a year later, on the next national holiday, the Prime Minister revoked the sentences of fifty prisoners – Rutiewa was one of them.

Another character, although this time a lovely one, was a little, very old lady who came to call soon after we arrived. She carried a live chicken, which she thrust in my hands, and immediately prostrated herself in front of me. Now I'm used to kissing and hugging, but this style of greeting bothered me. I tossed the chicken in Prosper's hands and hauled her up, telling Prosper to inform her never to bow before me again! That was the beginning of a lovely friendship.

She spoke only her own tribal language but even so, we understood and loved each other, babbling away in our own tongues. Every three or four days she'd pop in for tea and look at my photos or magazines, chuckling over the near-naked ladies. She was a potter, making her wares and firing them in a hillside kiln in the old fashion. She'd bring me pots of all shapes and I'd give her some sugar or shillings. Actually, I used some of the pots every day; they were marvelous for slow-cooking white beans or stew. I often think of the little granny now when I notice the pots I brought home.

It's very difficult to guess ages, as women tend to age fast in Africa, but her son told me she was born the year the locusts came! So your guess is as good as mine.

In the town of Sumbawanga we had some white friends, one of whom was a German schoolteacher there with the German volunteer service. Brigitta used to ride her little motorbike out to the ranch once or twice a week, usually on weekends. One day I saw her chugging up our hill and wondered what on earth was wrong. She had such a scowl on her pretty face, I thought something dreadful had happened. I ran out as she hopped off.

"I *refuse* to stay home. It's my birthday and I have no one to celebrate with!" She hauled her pack into the house and proceeded to unpack spaghetti, some tomato paste and a bottle of Dodoma wine. So the two of us had a party and talked half the night, with her leaving at five in the morning to get to school on time.

Brigitta had trouble accepting the style of punishment meted out by the teachers on their pupils, especially the girls. Even a teenage girl, if being punished, had to strip her drawers and bend over while the teacher caned her bottom, in front of all the other teachers. Brigitta was really horrified and I don't blame her.

Another couple very dear to us were Norwegian – Helge and Liv. Helge was a water engineer, a very handsome fellow with a Sir Walter Rawleigh beard. He had a military bearing, as well he should; he was an officer in the Norwegian reserve army. His wife Liv was just beautiful, tiny and dainty. She had been a ballerina in Norway. Their little daughter was just a year old when we arrived. When most children are just learning to speak, this child was learning Swahili and Norwegian as well as some English from me and a bit of German from Brigitta.

Because Bill was away so much, I spent a good deal of time with Helge and Liv. Helge would be off at his work in the jungles so Liv and I would devise various projects to work on together.

If it hadn't been for Helge and Carl Madsen, a missionary from Denmark, I never would have been able to open an account at the bank in Sumbawanga. Women, I was told, should not have accounts of their own! I needed one – Bill was away all the time and I had to have access to cash in order to look after things and travel to meet Beth and so on. I had Bill write a letter to the manager, but no dice. I filled out forms, forms and more forms and stood in line for hours, but they just didn't want me or my business. In desperation I went to Helge and he, along with Carl, dug out all the rubber stamps they had – stamps with their addresses, their work, their church – every single one. "Tanzanians love offical stamps, Bets!" I was told as I looked on in astonishment. They typed up a great letter stating my need of an account and vouching for my honesty and stamped it with every single stamp. Then we all piled in the Land Rover and down to the bank we went. I got my account!

When I broke my ankle, it was Helge and his men who made my crutches. Bill and Helge went hunting together whenever they could. One time they shot an old buffalo and proudly brought home the gigantic liver. We made liver pate' but it was so strong we couldn't eat it – even the dogs wouldn't touch it – but it was a wonderful hunt, we were told!

Helge was very capable, often accomplishing feats that

nobody in their right mind would attempt.

Once when he was out on safari, he met a native who was holding his hand in a blood-soaked rag. Helge examined it and found the thumb almost completely severed; it was attached by only a piece of skin. The man begged Helge to help him.

Helge opened his first aid kit and found a needle and heavy thread. He warned the fellow that infection would probably set in and he would lose the thumb anyway, but the man insisted. So Helge stitched it as best he could.

Months later he again met the man, who triumphantly showed him his hand. The thumb was slightly crooked, but he had retained the use of it.

Then there were Hingi and his wife Debbie. Hingi was the ranch manager at the Uvinza ranch, and he was a rascal. He used everyone and played the system like an old pro. But what finished me with Hingi was, one time I went to his place to see Debbie. There in his back porch were fifty or more cases of fish tinned in Germany, and stamped on each tin was "For refugee camps in Tanzania — a gift from Germany." To heck with the refugees — Hingi was selling them at a great profit!

Debbie was a lovely, gentle lady. She did beautiful embroidery work, without a pattern and with ordinary sewing thread. To decorate her house, she brought in creepers from the jungle and potted them, and they trailed over her doorway and windows. At her place I tasted my first cassava. This root is dug and peeled and boiled like a potato and actually tastes quite like it. Often, if I stopped for a cup of tea, she would place cold cassava on a plate like I would cookies for a treat.

One time, when I was up visiting Bill, Debbie came and asked me to do her hair like I did my own. Well, mine was shoulder-length, brown and straight except when I stuck my plastic curlers in it. Debbie had noticed me in my curlers and thought she'd like hers like that. Her hair was a real fuzzy Afro but as I tried to explain that it wouldn't work, I knew I wasn't getting through to her, so all I could do was try.

Up I went with my pink and green plastic curlers, and I dampened and I wound this very frizzy hair. What a job! I finally got it all wound up and waited for it to dry. The result was like nothing on earth! It stood out in all directions and looked absolutely ghastly. She looked in the mirror and told me rather shakily how nice it was, thank you, and I went back to the trailer.

That evening we were going to town. When Debbie got in the Land Rover she was wearing a kerchief. I peeked under it and saw that she had washed her hair and braided it. I was much relieved, but she felt a bit sheepish!

At the Uvinza ranch, the veterinarian was a tall handsome Masai chap. When I first met him he had recently married a girl from Mbeya who was a former prostitute. This bothered her and she was always wary of anyone who might have seen her soliciting.

One evening Bill and I were out for our evening stroll and I thought I heard music. Not African music, but – could it be – Jimmy Reeves? As we drew nearer I listened closely. Sure enough, it was Jimmy singing his heart out! It seemed Orio, the vet's wife, had two records – one of Jimmy Reeves and one of Dolly Parton. It gave me a strange nostalgic feeling to hear something here in the backwoods of Africa that I knew from back home.

About halfway through our two-year contract, a young vet arrived to assist Bill with his work with the cattle at the four ranches. Dr. Kessy was well-read, dedicated and optimistic. He had taken his training in Nairobi and was as qualified as his Canadian peers. Bill and I both felt that the hope of Africa lies in people like Dr. Kessy.

Beans Again!

At our headquarters at Sumbawanga, we always had enough to eat. But many times we found needed supplies unavailable.

Sumbawanga was not on the rail line and all supplies had to be freighted in by truck. Because of the roads, the vehicles and the weather, there were always shortages of something: cooking oil, margarine, sugar, flour or rice or any combination of these.

But I soon learned. You don't need three well-balanced meals a day to exist like we were used to back on the farm. Many times we would have just white beans and tomatoes grown right on the ranch for several days at a time. The white beans, cooked slowly with onion, tomatoes and the inevitable chili peppers, were a good enough meal.

I also learned to store away foodstuffs. When cooking oil and Tan Bond margarine were plentiful I'd buy extra, and the same with sugar. My closet had more food than clothing in it most of the time.

Improvisation was another skill I quickly acquired. In Canada, if I was about to bake and found I didn't have one ingredient, I'd either go to town for it or not bake. Here, if I found I had three of seven ingredients I was delighted and would bake madly. I remember making green tomato pickle with *red* tomatoes, white sugar, onions and vinegar – with a chili or two, of course!

Eggs were always a problem. Before we came, fowl cholera had swept through the area and killed off most of the chickens, so eggs were hard to get. I was often unlucky enough to buy eggs only to find they were absolutely rotten. So I turned all egg purchasing over to Prosper. He had all sorts of tests to see if an egg was fresh and if it wasn't, the Swahili really flew thick and fast. He definitely enjoyed the post of official egg tester, and we had a deal – a package of Safari cigarettes for six fresh eggs, which I paid for. That's how precious a good egg was to me at the time. But of course Safari cigarettes were dirt cheap – I had been told they were made of the sweepings at the end of the day at the factory. But when you consider that Jumamosi used to bum my old used tea leaves for a smoke, Safari cigarettes were quite acceptable!

I was very fortunate to have daughters at home as well as a good friend who sent me surprise packages every few months. Everything from yeast to yarn, thread and Toni kits were sent over, carefully sewn into little white sacks. I'd get them three months later, and mail days were the highlight of each week. (The day the sugar arrived ran a close second.)

If Beth was home we'd make tea and sit about, reading and re-reading all the letters half the night, pigging out on any food we received in the mail. The papers would be months old, but it was all fresh to us. (The only Canadian news we ever heard on the radio was "Margaret Trudeau Meets the Rolling Stones!")

Joyce and I had an unwritten agreement to test each other's recipes and strange dishes. I made scalloped potatoes one day and told her to try them. She thought they looked terrible. I explained that it was just milk, potato and onion, so she tentatively tried a wee bit – and ended up polishing off half the panful. But when I made some green Jello one day she couldn't try it. "Mama Beth, if I eat that I'll throw up!" And she meant it!

There were some things she cooked that I couldn't handle either. One was the stomach of a cow (it looks like seaweed, all green and wavy) and the other was the cow's hoof – stewed, hide, hair and all!

We did cook a lot of the local white beans and so did Joyce. But where I would add two chili peppers Joyce would add four or five – and if she was mad at Mbani she'd put in ten or more. They were even hotter than our chili peppers, so it must have really singed the hairs in his nose!

One thing all Tanzanians cook are chappatties. These thin, pancake-like breads can be cooked on an old pan over an open fire. The main recipe is just flour and water, although Joyce liked to add a little sugar and an egg if it was available. In Tanzania most people eat from a central bowl with their fingers, or using the chappatty as a bowl. (It is considered unclean to eat with your left hand. In fact, it is inexcusable to hand a person anything with your left hand. This was a bit difficult for me, being a lefty.)

Sugar was the one commodity the people would sell their souls for. Tanzanians love their tea made with part water and part milk, boiled and really laced with sugar. It took me a while to acquire a taste for it, but I got so I quite liked it. Joyce would make a big potful in the morning and put it in a couple of thermoses for the day.

I loved the marketplaces. They were noisy, cheerful and colorful. The village mamas would walk miles with their produce in baskets atop their heads – cabbages, bananas, tomatoes and even cape gooseberries. You could buy some strange things at the market – roasted termites, tiny fish the size of a dragonfly stinking to high heaven, and there was a special section just for the old tribal herbs and medicines. When in season, things were cheap – for five shillings you could buy a big brown bag of cape gooseberries which were delicious when boiled with sugar and water. Often I made them into jam.

All the little dukas which surrounded the market would stock other items. So, each time, you'd buy whatever fresh produce you could, then peek in all the other dukas to see what was interesting. If you noticed they had rice without too many stones or flour without weevils, you bought like crazy, delighted to have found such wonders. Of course if stones and weevils were part of the bargain and you were desperate, you bought some anyway and cleaned the stuff as well as you could at home. Beggars can't be choosers! In fact, each trip, you visited every store in the whole town – partly to socialize and partly to make sure you didn't miss something very wonderful like a can of orange juice.

One such trip, I discovered a tin of herrings in tomato sauce canned in Scotland. What a find! I hoarded them for a very special occasion, one which would have to be monumental! Finally, when Beth and Bill were home and we were having company for dinner, I decided the time was right. It wasn't a very big can but I didn't like fish, and it looked like just enough to serve our guests. However, we were out of propane at the time, so I had to cook the whole dinner on two kerosene burners. In desperation I thought I'd heat the fish in the fireplace — they didn't have to cook anyway, just warm up.

As I went on with my other preparations the mechanic's boy, who was home from boarding school, happened to be in the front room reading and noticed the tin nestled in the flames. He grabbed the Swahili-English dictionary and was busy looking up "heat expansion" when the thing blew. And boy, did it blow! Our ceilings were fourteen feet high and they were plastered with burning coals and bits of fish. Coals and cinders had been blown all over the room, into the sponge cushions and onto the mats, some still burning merrily.

Simba, who was working in his garden, heard the blast a mile away. His first thought was that Mbani, who was down at the bomas drinking with some town chaps, had shot someone in all the merrymaking. Meanwhile, poor Mbani thought Joyce had finally done in the visiting Sophia, as she had been threatening to do for weeks! What a hoorah it was! We ran around putting out the fires, sweeping up bits and pieces and airing out the house. The tin was found later at the bottom of the hill — the lid we never saw again.

We grew a bit of a garden on our terrace but we had to really work at it. The goats and the odd chicken were forever in them, and I'd be out chasing and yelling. This only worked a few times. Soon the goats got used to this apparition waving a broom and screeching; they'd just glance up and proceed as though I weren't there.

The odd human mishap would also happen from time to time. I couldn't grow peas, as the insects ate the seed before it had a chance to germinate, but I could grow whoppers of string beans. They really thrived in the African climate. One batch was absolutely perfect, green and succulent, just ready to bloom — my, I was smug. One morning I went out to gaze adoringly at them and to my horror, I beheld nothing but so many straight bare stalks! Someone had come in the night and stripped each and every leaf — Africans call anything green and leafy *spinachi*, and boil it to eat. This had been the fate of my poor beans.

Often I was asked for a head of lettuce which they would

also boil in the same manner. Of course, to all foodstuffs they'd add the ubiquitous chili peppers, or *pili pili* as they called them.

Every time we were in Mbeya I'd go to a store owned by a Goan. It was quite a large store but you would think by looking at his shelves that there was very little in it. But for a price and if he took a liking to you, it was amazing what he could find out back. One day I was sitting in there having a visit with his wife when I mentioned that what I missed most (that particular day – I was always missing something!) was perfume. My limited supply was gone and I felt almost naked without it. He went scurrying out back and came back with a bottle of French perfume! Vanity overcame me, I'm afraid, and I paid a fortune for it. Luxuries were few and far between in my new life!

Our meat was always available as the ranch butchered twice a week to sell in town at the market. We didn't have a fridge so I'd buy enough for three days and cook it all immediately. The odd time in the hot season some would spoil but it was never wasted. Prosper and his wife were not as fussy as I, so he'd take it home for supper very happily. But then Prosper would also eat the unformed eggs out of the inside of a chicken he was cleaning, and one time he took home a big mouse he found in my cupboard to eat too.

At the Uvinza ranch also, food was very scarce. Bill would be extremely hungry most of the time unless I was there to cook the inevitable beans. There was a little market in town but never any food, and only once in a while could he buy bread or cookies in a duka. He'd shoot game but was too busy to cook it. I sent Prosper with him on one trip and that worked fine. He cooked and kept up the laundry but when he came home after two months, he said he would *never* go back. "It's too much work, Mama Beth!" He felt he had to perform the duties Bill set out for him, whereas with me it wasn't so important to do as he was told. After all, I was white and a woman – why would you bother to be diligent for such?

Bill once shot a big bustard, a bird as big as our turkey. He could almost taste it! He gave it to someone to cook and they boiled it – not long enough. It was tougher than you can imagine, and tasteless. My, Bill was disappointed!

Tanzanian Women

The village women I met were basically hard-working, kind people. They had very little, many owning only one or two kangas, but they took pride in their children and were always singing and laughing.

I saw many different hairstyles – more intricate than anything Hollywood could dream up. Some would take hours and hours to achieve, but doing each other's hair was a social thing, so time didn't matter. Most of the styles involved making a thousand little spikes sticking at various angles over the head, or tiny braids so fine you could hardly see them. Joyce tried very hard to convince me to allow her to do mine but I worried I'd never get it picked out, as all the styles make use of fine thread interwoven amongst the strands of hair. I had visions of my hair falling out, and so chickened out.

The women, poor though they were, liked to decorate themselves and look good to each other. If they didn't own earrings they'd run a hoop of fine wire or colorful thread through the ear lobes.

Once, at home, some village ladies caught me before I managed to get my curlers out in the morning and they oohed and aahed admiringly, figuring I had put them in for decoration! But I had seen one lady with a pink diaper pin stuck dead centre in her hair for decoration, so I guess it's understandable!

Many of the ladies, as well as some of the men, had tribal scars made when they were little, usually by the witch doctors. This is done by cutting the skin with a chunk of iron and rubbing ashes in the wound. The ashes ensure a well-raised scar. The odd girl from a different tribe would have her front teeth filed to points, which they also thought quite alluring. The babies would often have strings of fine beads around their fat middles and wrists – partly for aesthetic value and partly to fend off evil spirits.

Sometimes, when Joyce and I were visiting a village, dancing would start. The women all danced together while the men were off somewhere drinking or talking, and I would inevitably be dragged up rather reluctantly. However, my dancing, like my Swahili, was a source of much amusement. They expected me to bend in places I didn't have joints and I came off not unlike a strutting ostrich. At first Joyce thought my shoes were causing the trouble but even when I kicked them off, I couldn't wiggle like they did. Finally, with great merriment, it was decided it was my skin — white skin must just be too stiff to bend like their supple flesh! But we always had a great time, dancing or no dancing.

Joyce and I went to a nearby village once and found that a wedding had just taken place. When we arrived, the bride was waiting at her parents' home for the groom to take her to their new hut. I noticed her sitting in a corner in a white dress, but instead of the happy smiling bride I expected, I found a very sorrowful-looking girl with her face half covered as though in shame. I figured she was afraid of the marriage bed or sorry to leave her mother, so of course I clucked like a mother hen and tried to tell her marriage was a wonderful adventure and by tomorrow she'd be on cloud nine at least!

Joyce hustled over and whispered, "Leave her be, Betty. Don't say anything!" I knew enough to do as Joyce said. She had eased me out of other mistakes I had made.

On the way home, Joyce explained with great patience. "It's our tradition, Mama Beth. The bride never looks happy. If she looks too happy, her husband might not pay all the bride price, and if she cries enough, he just might give her father an extra goat or two!"

There are little one-room schools in most of the large villages, with some good teachers and some poor like everywhere else in the world. These teachers (the ones I met) were local girls who had finished about grade eight themselves and were not yet married. The children everywhere wore uniforms, all made of a special cotton twill in four basic colors — blue, green, white or yellow. The girls' uniforms were little jumpers, worn with white blouses or without, and the boys had white shirts and shorts. They would be made by the innumerable sewers who sat with their treadle machines on the sidewalks of Sumbawanga.

Each family included not only Mom and Dad, but extra

wives, all the kids, the odd grandma or grandpa, nieces and nephews. All helped with the chores, which were basic and hard, but there were usually so many in the family, it was well-divided.

There was one quirk of the village women that I never could quite figure out. Every once in a while, say every seven or eight months, one would go away to a far-off village or to her former home. Now, that in itself is not so strange; but when I'd ask her husband or mother where she was, they would point to their heads and say, "Sick, Mama, sick!" And, sure enough, it was true. Many of the village women became unbalanced to the point where you couldn't get through to them. They would be sent off for a rest and this did seem to work – in every case, the woman would be home after a month or two, quite normal once again.

I never figured out whether they were really having mental problems, or they simply needed a change and were consummate actresses!

Homes which contained more than one wife were often very stormy. The men – even the well-educated ones in town – extolled the virtues of having two or three wives. The hospital administrator would argue with me every time we met – or maybe I argued with him!

"Mama Beth, our wives like us to have more than one. They have someone to visit with and someone to share the chores," he'd say. "They are very happy with this system!" But I saw so much grief and heartache caused by his great system, he could never convince me of its worth. In all the time I was there, I never once heard a woman say she was happy her husband had two or three wives. In fact, there was many a royal battle between wives. I treated gashes in heads caused by one wife lobbing something at another. I used to think they should have pooled that strength and anger together at the blooming man! He caused the grief!

Joyce was devastated when Mbani took Sophia as his second wife. All the Tanzanians I met around the area had mistresses all over the place, and that was bad enough, but to bring her legally home and tell his wife to be good to her was a bit much!

Mbani was later to take two of the children, the two boys, and go with Sophia to another posting at a different ranch. Joyce was left to fend for herself and little Mary, later having another little girl she named Betty.

I think there's hope for a better life for the village women, though. One time all the workers' wives and the nearby village ladies were hired to clean the corrals. To accomplish this they had to fill baskets with the manure, and carry them on their heads out to the maize patch and dump them. The corrals were huge and it was dirty, hard work. By the middle of the day the ladies had got their heads together and decided to revolt. Either they would get more shillings or they'd quit – let the men clean the corrals by hand! It wasn't a peaceful strike either! They all marched up the great hill to the offices, trilling and war-whooping as only African ladies can, getting more boisterous each step of the way.

The men were all afraid of the mob but Mr. Kingazi, the veterinarian and peacemaker at the ranch, finally got up enough nerve to go out and meet with them. They got their raise too! This tiny bit of·courage on their part, demanding their rights, made me think that if they could all band together over the whole country, they could demand that the government change the laws that discriminate against women.

The ladies are also very kind. While we were in Africa, we lost a member of our family back home. I was alone at the ranch when the phone call came from Dar – Bill was at Uvinza and Beth at school. I was in shock, but by the time I got back to the house, Joyce was there and Prosper had the tea brewing. All that day the "coconut telegraph" worked, and ladies from the villages surrounding the ranch, as well as the workers' wives, came by twos and threes, their kangas over their faces as a sign of sorrow, and sat with me. I was never alone the whole of the day.

The next day the men all came, and to top this off a collection was taken and given to us by the workers. It wasn't much, but it was from people who had next to nothing, and they cared and showed they cared. I think we bought something for the children to play with on the ranch later, but I'll never forget their kindness to us at the time. Each time I go to send a card to someone in sorrow now, I think of my Tanzanian friends and their love.

Mechanic's wife at Uvinza, sporting a common Tanzanian hairstyle.

Roads could be unpredictable in the wet season!

The cantankerous buffalo. While you stalk it, it often stalks you!

Joyce Mbani, dressed and posing!

Young children carried everything on their heads,
even up and down our high hill.

Bill and his guide atop Kilimanjaro after a three-day climb.

Kilimanjaro peeping through the clouds, as seen from Arusha.

*My good friend who crafted clay pots,
shown here with her granddaughter.*

*Prize bull all ready to show at the Saba Saba Day celebrations.
George is at the halter with Rutiewa looking on.*

Dancing celebrates the end of Ramadan in Sumbawanga.

Celebrations

The people seem to love celebrations, and it takes very little to start the drums rolling. It was a rare night when I wasn't lulled to sleep by the sound of drums in the villages below.

Besides Ramadan and Christmas, the really big holiday in Tanzania is Saba Saba Day, the Tanzanian independence day. It is planned for months ahead and is actually the Tanzanian version of our old-time country fair.

Booths were set up, some built of homemade brick, and goods were sold by all the mission stations, the refugee camps, the ranch – even the prison had a booth. The inmates grew the most wonderful onions and carrots, and made basic furniture for sale.

The ranch erected its own booth, and started its preparations three months ahead. Bill decided we would show some livestock, as is done at the Regina Fair or the Calgary Bull Sale. They picked out a bull, a steer and a heifer. The cattle were nearly all Zebu, the ordinary African breed, with the odd Boran one. Once the choice was made – quite a job in itself as there were about four thousand head to choose from – Bill went to town for a good rope to make halters. There was little choice – actually, no choice – a poor-quality sisal was all they had.

Now any rancher can tell you, it isn't everyone who can make a good halter. You need your wife's good sewing shears, a sharp knife and a heavy boot. Also, I've noticed, you need a good lot of spit. I think the more spit the better, with lots of noise mixed in! I have watched the performance of halter-making for years, but Bill had the ranch workers absolutely mesmerized!

Once the halters were complete, we all trooped down the hill where they instantly transformed three docile creatures into holy hellers! The animals had never seen a halter before and it took days to calm them and longer to teach them to lead properly. After much work and many bruises to body and spirit, the animals were docilely walking along behind the men. George, one of the cattlemen, asked Bill in great seriousness, "Is this how you teach camels to lead in Canada?"

Close to the day, my second-best hairbrush disappeared along with all the Vaseline from the duka, and the animals were groomed like they were members of the Royal Family. They did look magnificent – the Queen Mum would have loved them! While Bill was busy with the stock, I was busy sewing chuppies. Chuppies are underpants for children, made in any material of every conceivable size and worn by all and sundry. My, I had some brilliant ones. These were for my friends, the Moravian missionaries, to sell at their booth.

The ranch butchered two animals which were cooked on a fire at the ranch booth, and the meat was sold on sticks throughout the day.

It was an unwritten law that everyone had to wear their very best clothes – it didn't matter if you were spending the day in a rough, dusty sportsground. I had no choice – high-heeled white sandals and a pastel blue dress. No pants today for the Mama!

The ladies all wore their brightest kangas and what a colorful sight it was – every shade imaginable sweeping along, black-eyed babies peeking out from their perches on the mamas' backs.

There were marching bands and soldiers doing field exercises, and political speeches which droned on and on as we sat on the ground listening to each try to outdo the last.

Once that part was over, we were free to walk around to all the booths and visit, chewing away on a chunk of goat meat. There were a few tribal dance displays which I just loved. The innumerable pombi booths were the busiest and happiest spots!

It was a tired lot who finally got home to the ranch about eight at night, but a good time was had by all, some not returning for two days!

Another big festival is celebrated by the Muslims at the end of their month of fasting. It too can go on for days on end.

Christmas is very like ours, except they do not give presents. The Christians go to church services and the rest hit the pombi – not unlike Canada.

Our first Christmas there I'll never forget. I knew long before

December I would find it strange, but I didn't realize how very different. One warm day I was sweeping my patio and suddenly realized it was the end of October. It took over a month to send a letter home and I hadn't even thought about Christmas, never mind cards. Back in Canada, I'd have had my baking in the freezer and some of the shopping done. But then, in Canada I'd have had snow and TV commercials to remind me!

I got dressed up (which meant wiping the red dust off my toes and throwing on a clean cotton skirt and a dash of cologne) and grabbed my purse. I hopped into the Land Rover and went to town for cards. Of course I could find none – a lot of shops were run by Muslims and they didn't believe in Christmas, and the others said no one could afford cards so they didn't stock them. I was out of luck.

Then I remembered Carl and Rigmor, our Danish friends. They were methodical, organized and helpful – I counted on all three. Sure enough, they had sent all their cards and had a hundred and fifty left! I traded them a chunk of beef and some wilted beets for my precious cards.

These cards were aerograms, with a tiny Christmas motif on the top and a great blank space below to write wonderful Christmas thoughts on. Fine, but at home all I ever wrote on a Christmas card was something like "Merry Christmas – will write soon!" and here I had seven inches of paper to fill! As I sat at my desk with the cards about me, I wrote little nothings like "the birds are singing, the flowers are in full bloom and it certainly doesn't seem like Christmas!"

But I soon forgot all about my brilliant prose as I felt a hearty sting on my ankle, and another and another. I looked down and saw, to my horror, that army ants had invaded my home, my hearth and my clothing!

Now if you've ever read about army ants and their ability to maim, kill and destroy, it's all true. They run right up your body, and before you know it, you're covered. The only way to dislodge them is to strip and pick each one off separately and this you'll find you can accomplish very quickly – their bite is dreadful and you forget all about modesty.

Army ants sweep in a formation about two feet wide and crawl over anything in their path. They are very hard to discourage and here they were wandering through my house. Prosper came running on my first shriek and we spent the whole day trying to get rid of them. Fly spray did absolutely nothing. Then we tried hot ashes from the fireplace and even the blowtorch. Still they kept coming. Finally we got some of the chemical used in the cattle dip and poured it on them full strength. This didn't kill them, but they did slouch off.

Soon it was time to meet Beth in Mbeya as she would be home for Christmas holidays. I took all my cards with me, planning on addressing them on the long bus ride there.

On the way, we had to get off the bus at the bottom of a long high hill and I walked up, carrying my precious cards. Just as I got to the top, a good Rift Valley wind whipped them out of my hand and swept them aloft. By the time I got them collected, a goat and three kids had got hold of some of them and they looked like it. Then farther on, a baby sat on them and I was forced to air them out the window the rest of the way. I did get them mailed off, however, along with a fervent prayer to high heaven to please place understanding hearts in all who were to receive my tattered, mucky greetings from faraway Africa.

It wasn't long until Christmas week. Beth and I were a bit homesick, but we figured we'd give the holiday season the very best we had. A good friend had sent a fruitcake mix and I made it up. Beth bought a big bag of groundnuts and roasted them and made peanut brittle, peanut brownies and anything else calling for peanuts in our recipe box. We made fancy buns and a bit of white fudge.

Next on our list was a Christmas tree. I'm sure we could have lived without a tree but we longed for familiarity. So, armed with my one good butcher knife, we went out searching. We were lucky; the Germans had planted trees which resembled our cedars and we picked a small one. It took a while, but we finally got it chewed off with the knife and we lugged it back to the house, proud as all get out.

Now we had to decorate it. CUSO volunteers travel light and have little room for such things as Christmas decorations, so we improvised. The old cupboards were held shut with bits of colored tape, so we swiped it and tied it in bows here and there. Beth cut out paper snowflakes but it still looked bare. We went to the duka in search of what, we weren't sure. Lo and behold, there tucked at the back were three bags of candy made in China. The candy was old and hard but each one was wrapped in gold-colored foil! We tied them all on our tree and sat back, very impressed.

Next, what would we eat in place of turkey? The ducks and geese had all died of cholera, but there was the odd chicken about. So I sent Prosper off to find a chicken for us. What a day he had! He came back reeling with happiness and pombi, clutching one skinny chicken. I'm not sure I made a great deal – I paid a hundred shillings and a carton of cigarettes – but we'd have roast chicken for dinner.

Prosper fell asleep on the back step and Beth and I were left to deal with the live chicken. Now, I had seen chickens butchered but had never tried it myself. Beth said she'd hold it if I chopped its head off, so we laid it out on an old stump, Beth hanging on for dear life with her eyes shut. I looked down and found it staring back at me, so I laid a dishtowel over its head and brandished my dull butcher knife. Just as I was getting down to business I was called to the phone. I glanced up, Beth let go of the chicken and it streaked for freedom! It was our Danish friends calling to ask if we'd like to come to the closest village, where they were holding a Christmas service, and then to their place for Danish Christmas supper. Would we!

There was still one worry, however. Bill planned on being home Christmas Eve but it was the rainy season and we hadn't heard from him. It was very likely he could have road trouble and not get home.

By nine-thirty Christmas Eve we had the tree all aglow, our gifts were wrapped and we sat back waiting. We had made up our minds that if he didn't make it, we'd celebrate ourselves as best we could. But all of a sudden this handsome head flipped by the window – Bill was home!

After he took a quick shower, we all sat and opened our gifts: a plastic-handled jackknife for Beth, who was our chronic tomboy, books for Bill and zebra-skin thongs for me. After hot chocolate and much chatter, we settled down for the night.

Christmas morning we walked to the village and greeted all our friends. In the little mud church everyone sat on three-legged stools or the floor. It had been decorated for the occasion; wild flowers were placed in a rusty tin on the homemade pulpit and others were placed in an old Dr. Chase's liniment box which hung from the ceiling.

The service started and my thoughts wandered back home to my own family. I wondered how they were and where they were celebrating Christmas Day. But before I could become morose the singing began; and although the words were all in Swahili, the music was the same as the carols at home. We went through the whole lot – Away in a Manger, O Little Town of Bethlehem, Silent Night. It was a moving moment.

After the service we were all invited to the head elder's hut for *ugali* and goat meat. It was simple, eaten from a central bowl, but it was all they had and it was served with love.

Later, we went on into town for our traditional supper and a visit. That night, after Beth and Bill were asleep, I sat out on the big back steps and relaxed, thinking over the day's events. The stars were brilliant – were they really closer here on my African hill? They seemed so.

As I looked up, I couldn't help but feel transported in time. Those same stars shone long ago on a tiny Child, one who was born to save the whole world – both Eastern and Western, all cultures and creeds.

Our second Christmas was a disaster in some ways, but interesting in others. Beth and I had gone up to the Uvinza ranch to visit Bill, and the three of us would come home to Liv and Helge's for Christmas Eve. Of course, it being the rainy season, the inevitable happened – we were marooned.

Christmas Eve found us at the club at the salt mine at a dance of sorts. Christmas Day we spent at Hingi and Debbie's eating goat meat and rice. Debbie had decorated her little house with huge leaves with tiny wildflowers stuck through the centre of them and it was very pretty.

New Year's still found us marooned, but this time we were up at the new headquarters in Bill's little trailer munching on impala that Beth had shot and green mango sauce. Needless to say, we weren't really ushering in the New Year with great merriment!

No, for real celebrating it took the village people. A new baby, a new calf, a rain when needed – anything would start the celebration. If I stopped to see a sick child or brought a gift to someone, they would start dancing or playing the drums. If I was hemming kangas at my house for a group of ladies, they'd sing and dance in time to the sewing machine. I'd swear they'd celebrate if the sun rose or if it didn't. Joyce said when I told her this, "If we sing and dance, then we are happy. Why be sad, Mama Beth?"

She had a very good point.

Holiday Time

While we were in Tanzania, the three of us were separated a great deal of the time. Beth and I could get together every three months but often we would not see Bill for months on end, and then only for short periods. But we did manage a few trips together which I will always cherish.

There were the annual CUSO meetings for all the Tanzanian volunteers and we were fortunate to attend three of these, since there was one held while we were still in Dar before leaving for our posting.

All CUSO personnel and volunteers would meet for two or three days, usually at some resort place, and hold meetings, bask in relative luxury and in general lick our wounds! I don't remember anything very earth-shaking ever being decided at these workshops – although I'm sure some of the other volunteers would disagree with me – but it was comforting to discuss our various problems, figure out our priorities and eat, drink and be merry.

These meetings also allowed us to view various projects, both governmental and voluntary, like the Ujimma Village government project, as well as various women's projects. The Ujimma Villages were very popular at the time. Government leaders would select a suitable area and a group of people to set up a sort of colony for collective farming, with a strong village government committed to the whole. Some were quite successful, but others were not.

We toured some very successful women's projects where they made and sold their own crafts, including tie-dyeing and weaving.

It was at the annual meetings where personal problems were handled. If a volunteer or a spouse became too homesick and wanted to terminate the contract, it was decided there whether CUSO would pay the return fare or not.

CUSO, I might add, has a wonderful track record and was sympathetic in most cases. If one were to find any fault at all

103

with the system, it might be in the selection and briefings of volunteers. But it's very difficult to judge how someone fresh and full of fervor to save the masses is going to react to his or her first Third World experience. I doubt there's anything one could tell new volunteers that would prepare them for this shock.

I did notice that many volunteers were devastated not so much by conditions as by their feelings of ineffectiveness. You soon learn – or else you fly home – that you may never see any improvements, you may never accomplish anything except mundane things, and you'll never be told how wonderful you are, by either the government or the people. (Would *you* heap praise on someone who came from afar expressly to change your ways, even if it were for the better?) You have to be open and learn as much from the people as they will from you; then you'll find you are accepted, and then you'll progress in your work – although, I must admit, *slowly*.

I especially found our field staff officers, Richard and Kleist, very helpful. No matter how mundane my problems were or how catastrophic, they had an answer – either a sympathetic ear or material help. And I've got to admit I hit them with everything – from sending me boracic acid to paying for my trips to meet and take Beth back and our two- or three-day stay in the city. Each time any of us was in Dar, we would end up at the cramped little CUSO office for a visit with the boys or Milly, the secretary.

The three of us had a full month's holiday halfway through our posting. It was wonderful. Beth was out for holidays and Bill had a month coming, so we went to Dar first, but instead of staying in a hotel we stopped at a fellow volunteer's home. His wife was home in Canada, so we just moved in for a few days. (It was common practice among the volunteers to stay with whoever lived in the place you were visiting.) His apartment was lovely, air conditioning and all. My, what luxury! (Of course, air conditioning or a good fan was vital in Dar – it was so hot and humid, the nights as hot as the day.)

We then took a small plane over to Mafia Island, situated about eighty miles off Dar mainland. The island is a real tropical paradise which boasts great swordfishing.

We stayed at a tourist fishing lodge, drinking in the beauty and peace. It was covered with palm trees and flowering shrubs and had a wonderful beach of white sand. We went fishing twice, which was fun if not successful. We caught only one measly foot-long fish – certainly not the monster I had envisioned catching. But we gave it to the chef who cooked it for supper with a great flourish.

Today, as has been true for the past three thousand years, trade is the lifeblood of the coastal towns of East Africa. Part of this commerce is still carried out by the Arabian dhows, the little wooden boats whose design has changed very little through the centuries. The dhows used to carry slaves and large quantities of gold; today they take ivory and wood from East Africa in exchange for carpets, fine chests and jewellery. Bill took pictures of the dhows we saw off Mafia Island, which the merchants certainly discouraged, shaking their fists and yelling at him. (I had found at Sumbawanga that the people were very hesitant to let us take photos when we first got there, especially if they were doing some mundane labor. They were afraid we would take the pictures home and laugh at their ways of doing things. But by the time we left, we had people lining up to have their pictures taken – usually holding my typewriter case and our little radio – as status symbols, I guess.)

After our island stay, we took the bus up to Moshi where Beth went to school. I couldn't get over the contrast between Sumbawanga area and Moshi and Arusha. The main tribe in the Moshi-Arusha area is the Chagga tribe which is by far the most advanced in Tanzania. They live on the forested slopes of Mount Kilimanjaro which has good rich soil that they use to their advantage, growing crops and raising cattle.

Although there is a heavy rainfall there, it comes in spits and spats, so this tribe developed a very complex system of irrigation. These channels can run for several miles, over ridges and down valleys, taking water from permanent water streams to drought areas. The Chaggas at one time lived on their income from bananas and cattle. But just after World War I, Sir Charles Dundas was placed in charge of the Chagga territory. He soon noticed how suitable the soil was for growing coffee, so he showed them how they could plant coffee under the banana trees, using the leaves to shelter the coffee plants from the hot sun. It worked very well and the Chaggas never looked back, building the largest co-operative in all of East Africa, collecting, processing and marketing their produce.

This is also the area of the Masai tribe – the last of the great warriors, they are called. On the streets of Moshi and Arusha you will always see the Masai people. But one time Bill and I were on a train heading home when a small band of Masai got on, both warriors and the women. They were most intriguing.

They are a transient tribe, moving with their cattle from pasture to pasture, roaming most of the year. The men are tall and slender, with finer features than a lot of the Bantu tribes. The men wear black gowns with a red blanket thrown over their shoulders. Both the men and the women had holes about the size of a nickel through their ear lobes, as well as through the top part of their ears. From these holes hung great colored hoops, some touching their shoulders. The men's hair was quite long, some almost shoulder-length, and looked for all the world like knitting yarn that was the color of the red clay of Africa. (In fact, I believe that's how it was achieved – by rubbing the soil into their hair with water.)

All their spears and guns as well as some knives were taken by the soldiers on the train when the group got on. Two men who sat with Bill were as intrigued with him as he was with them. They'd pinch his skin, pull the hairs on his arms and desperately tried to bribe him out of his jackknife. One fellow, who seemed to be a chief, was absolutely majestic. He had his hair short and clean and he cut a striking figure as he organized the seating for all the ladies. They were shorter than the men and had their heads shaved, but were really quite pretty even though bald. They had the black gowns and wore bracelets halfway up their arms. One or two of the mamas carried large gourds which I imagine contained one of the staples of their diet – a mixture of blood from their cows and smoky milk.

While we were in Moshi we visited Beth's school, and what a setting for a school! Just nestled at the bottom of Mount Kilimanjaro – or at least it certainly dominated the view. The school was a wonderful experience for Beth. There were about twenty different nationalities represented, just amongst the teachers. It was run in the British Form style and Beth found it much more advanced than at home. She also found she worked a lot harder. They had a great time, though. Horses were kept for riding and she remembers going for early-morning rides near the coffee plantations. They'd partly climb the mountain and do all sorts of wonderful extra activities. The pupils were all there because their parents were posted in the country, and they supported each other in everything. They made friends of all nationalities – a real learning experience.

The town of Arusha is settled at the foot of Mount Meru or Socialist Peak, as it's officially known. It is the headquarters of the Arusha tribe which are close relatives of the Masai. But the members of this tribe are primarily settled agriculturists, mostly growing maize, and you can see the gathered cobs hanging from trees and posts in the area to dry.

I really cut loose with my shopping in Arusha – it's set up for tourists, which I was at that time. I couldn't send the ivory rings out of the country, but I did get the authentic Masai spears which a native had brought in to barter for a few shillings. They had some made just for tourists, but I wanted the real McCoy.

But what we had really come to the area for was the mountain! Kilimanjaro has probably been filmed more, had more written about it, and appeared in more fiction than any other mountain on earth. And well it should. It is spectacular. The Masai believe the mountain bears God's throne at the top, and hold it in fear.

It's three and one-half miles high, or 19,340 feet, but you can walk up. Many mountaineers say it's not the hardest mountain to climb, but it is by far the most beautiful. I had broken my ankle so didn't try, but Bill thoroughly enjoyed the climb. There were five guides – I think one for each climber. They carried everything – white table linens and silver included.

The ascent of Kibo, the main peak, can be taken during any month, but January, July and October provide the best conditions. The first part of the climb passes through Chagga territory, then through forest where if you're lucky you'll catch a glimpse of black and white Colobus monkeys. The first night is spent at Mandera hut, just at the top of the forest.

The second day is over open moorland, an eleven-mile hike to Horombo hut which sits at 11,000 feet above sea level. Near the end of this stage of the climb, the air starts to thin and altitude sickness starts to affect you if it's going to. Your feet feel like lead and a lot of the climbers have headaches.

The third day is a nine-mile hike across the saddle between Kibo peak and Mawenzi to Top hut, 16,000 feet above sea level. This is surrounded by gigantic brown boulders lying every which way, as though the devil had abandoned a game of marbles.

But the real ordeal is still ahead. You're awakened at three in the morning to slip and slide to Gilman's Point in time for sunrise, and it's all worthwhile. Many climbers stop here but Bill continued to the very top, a two-hour walk around the rim of the two-mile-wide crater to Uhuru Point, the summit of Africa. President Nyerere placed a tablet there, when Tanzania got its independence, on which is written:

> We, the people of Tanganyika, would like to light a candle and put it on top of Kilimanjaro which would shine beyond our borders, giving hope where there was despair, love where there was hate and dignity where before there was only humiliation.

The altitude sickness I mentioned might just be a headache and nausea, but the odd person is affected with a more serious condition of the chest and lungs. This is what happened to Beth partway up – probably because she had quite a chest cold before starting. The solution was to bring her down in a hurry. It took two days and a visit from the current boyfriend on his motorbike to restore her health!

While Bill was climbing the mountain I stayed below at the little English-style lodge. It was no great hardship; the lodge was peaceful and had the loveliest rose garden you ever saw. The food was wonderful and Beth and I shopped, ate, talked and slept at night beneath the thick hyrax blankets which adorned each bed.

When our month was up we each went our separate ways – Beth to school, Bill to his ranches and I to the big old house at Sumbawanga – all replenished in body and spirit for the rest of our assignment.

A Day at the Ranch

An average day in my life at the ranch would run like this:

7 a.m. Oh, there's Prosper banging away downstairs. He must have won at cards last night – he's whistling! I head downstairs – it's a beautiful day.

A quick cup of tea and my first patient is here. A young boy was playing with an old board last night and has a long sliver. He's scared – it's his first visit. Prosper teases him while I find the tweezers, bandage and peroxide. I notice as I wash it that infection has started; out comes the sliver and he wants to keep it! He goes merrily on his way. Next, two village women, one with a burn on her leg where she bumped on a hot stone. It's already healing and the skin isn't broken, so a cup of tea and a dash of powder is all that's needed.

Prosper is busy sweeping up, but leaves to see if the duka's open yet. Back he comes with the message, "The Land Rover is going to town with the meat – in ten minutes, Mama!"

The secretary pops in with a letter for me to type in English. It'll have to wait until tonight. I hurry and put on a clean skirt and blouse and make-up. (I did use make-up every day – partly to keep myself happy and partly so I wouldn't scare my new friends!)

Just as I'm locking the door, Mbani hurries up. "Betty, we're having four men from the World Bank visit us in two days' time. Can you please entertain them?"

"Entertain? Like what?"

"Dinner at six, and drinks before and after please, if you can!"

Wow. I jot down some of the things I'll need – and hope I'll find – in town. Joyce comes hurrying – "Come on, Betty, they are waiting." As we arrive at the edge of the market I notice the jacarandas are in full bloom. Such a lovely blue!

Joyce and I hit the market first to buy our fresh produce before it's picked over. As I buy, I tell Joyce what I'd like to serve

111

our guests. Some hope, we both figure!

We're in luck today. There's good fresh flour and a shipment of Tan Bond – the best margarine. After we buy the staples, we stop for a Coke. What a treat – you can't often get it. We sit on an old step and relax.

Next we decide to see if there are any new kangas in – we each pick out two. Soon it's lunchtime and we go to the guest house run by a Somalian. They have just made some fresh *somosis* – the lovely little pastry filled with ground beef and spices. I buy extra to eat tonight! Prosper comes in, takes my bags and informs me there's good rice at the Arab's store.

Next I pick up the konyagi – the Tanzanian gin. Mbani said he'd get the beer for the men.

By the time we collect all the mamas that came with us, it's three o'clock. Simba the driver is in high spirits, though. He's been drinking with the men. As we drive home I quiz Prosper – do you think you can find me two or three chickens? I want to have chicken curry for the visitors. He thinks he might, so we drop him off at Essessa village to check around.

At home I collapse for a moment, then put everything away. By then the mail has been sorted and they bring mine. I get a letter from Beth, one from Bill who has been delayed yet another week, and three from Canada.

I type the letter from the office and take it over. On the way back I meet Lkanga who tells me Joyce wants me, so I go up to her house. There's a lady from town there who works at the hospital. She wanted to meet me – boy, what a hairdo! It must have taken hours to do!

By seven I realize Prosper won't be home tonight. He must have met some of his cronies in the village. At seven-thirty I'm all set for the night watchman to pop in to tell me he's going to turn the generator on – he does this each night, always stopping for tea and supper. He's never hungry, but he eats each time anyway!

By ten I'm in bed, still planning my menu: curry and rice, fresh bread, salad and that pudding powder Leona sent me, with cape gooseberries on top. If Prosper finds the chickens!

Bill's Contribution

I begged Bill to write a short chapter for those who, I am sure, wonder what he did on his posting. (Lest you think I hogged the book, keep in mind that I had to nag him, as only I can nag, for even this much – be thankful for small mercies!)

In 1976 I was posted by CUSO to the Tanzania National Ranching Company Ltd. (NARCO) as a Ranch Technical Officer. This challenging work, on a two-year contract, was to prove to be the most rewarding experience of my life.

NARCO at that time was the largest ranching operation on the African continent. Possibly it still is. With fifteen ranches throughout the country and five more proposed projects, they had a total herd of over one hundred thousand head of cattle grazing on 1.8 million acres. NARCO headquarters was in the capital city of Dar es Salaam and the ranches were divided into the four zones of the country.

I was assigned to the smallest and least developed zone, the southern one, which (for me) was lucky as it was very much a wilderness area. Of the four ranches in this zone, two were on the Ufipa plateau – highland grass. Sumbawanga ranch, our headquarters, with the buildings at 7,500 feet, was a well-developed ranch by African standards – with no horses and no fences, as was the case with all of them.

Kalambo ranch, about thirty-five miles away on the headwaters of the Kalambo River, was similar but a lot more swampy, which was a blessing in the dry season. Usangu ranch, out from Mbeya, was very different as it lay down in the Rift valley. In the dry season, it reminded me of the thorn scrub areas bordering African deserts. But in the rainy season, it had unbelievable grass growth. The most successful crop is rice, whereas maize is the staple of the other ranch areas of Sumbawanga and Kalambo. Usangu ranch covered a traditional grazing area of the Wasakumi, a Bantu tribe which has herded cattle here for centuries.

Six hundred miles away, on a tributary of the great

Malagarazi River at Uvinza, was my favorite of the four ranches. It was just being developed in a tsetse fly area. Until modern technology had somewhat controlled the tsetse fly problem, no cattle would have survived here. Uvinza ranch would have been any cattle rancher's dream – miles of black cotton soil (a western Canadian's gumbo) with grass not stirrup high, but higher than a horse. It was supporting huge herds of buffalo, Eland and Korongo and all sorts of smaller gazelles and wart hogs. Even lions and elephants were pests by their presence.

Cattle herds in this zone were based on the local East African Zebu, a small (about five hundred pound, less than four feet at the withers) humped beast that the ranching company was upgrading very quickly by using improved Borans. The management of cattle on all four ranches included herding them by day and corraling them in bomas at night. Weekly in the dry season and twice a week in the wet season, they had to be driven through a dip of acaricidal solutions to rid them of ticks. Ticks carry East Coast fever and, even more deadly at the Uvinza ranch, *nagana* or sleeping sickness.

Tsetse flies suck blood from game animals (which are carriers though they are immune to the diseases) and transmit the trypanosomes to the cattle. Trypanosomes can be seen through a microscope in the blood of cattle. I won't soon forget being asked my opinion of a blood sample on a slide at Uvinza. Confessing that I had experience with neither microscopes nor trypanosomiasis was like confessing I had no cattle experience!

However, I was able to help them increase calf crops by introducing the feeding of cotton cake to breeding herds in the dry season. The ranching company had a real problem with lactating cows not conceiving because of malnutrition, resulting in calving only every second year.

One of the things I was soon confronted with was having to do things that western Canadian farmers would trust only to outside help. For example, only vets use live virus vaccines in immunizing for brucelosis in Canada, but administering strain-19 vaccine was often my job in Africa. I was designing water catchment structures such as earth dams and charcos (dugouts) which we in western Canada depend on government engineers to design. I found myself showing them how to key out the sub-soil for a dam, or even how to get the tracks back on a D7G Caterpillar.

I have mentioned only the things I was showing them, when actually I was able to learn far more than I taught. The people I worked and lived with in East Africa were unbelievably helpful in teaching me how to cope with cattle ranching in the tropics. When given half a chance, the natives of this area will be able to produce beef in abundance. It is terribly underdeveloped but the soil and climate, as well as the people themselves, are capable of a progress that will eventually make western Canada seem the difficult place to produce beef. Especially with our winters!

Farewell, Dear Friends

Our two years at times seemed to creep along, if I was alone for any length of time or if nothing much was doing, but this was seldom. Time whizzed by, and when plans had to be made for our departure it seemed impossible to believe it was over.

Beth and I found ourselves with the proverbial woman's complaint: "Not a thing to wear home!" But in our case it was true. We had just about worn out the clothes we had arrived with and what was left was so worn with washing by hand and the hot African sun, it was almost in rags. The elastic in our underwear was stretched out and our feet hurt in shoes after wearing thongs for two years.

So, for two months or more we'd write home, "What are the fashions at home this year? What is the current dress length?" Now we might have been placed at the back of beyond but, by golly, we wanted to make a grand entrance on our return!

We schemed and planned. We'd fly out in our old duds but boy, when we hit Europe — but in order to buy the elegant outfits we saw in our dreams we'd need money. I was afraid I wouldn't be in Dar long enough to buy travelers' cheques so I sent a cheque home and had the girls send me several hundred-dollar bills. They knew their mother too well so didn't bother explaining that it was a hare-brained, addle-pated idea. They just sent them in some cards. In one mail delivery I got a birthday card, a get-well card and three sympathies! I hid my loot a different place each day, often forgetting the last spot and giving myself heart failure three times a week. This money I papered on my stomach for the flight. Was I relieved when the plane took off!

We packed up what we were taking and dispensed with the rest. We started packing our crate early, and with each addition I'd weep and each time Joyce and I met we'd weep — I think if we looked up the rainfall on the hill for April 1978, it would have been increased by three inches over the average.

The workers and villagers put on a great farewell held at our house. There was goat meat, pombi and speeches by the dozens. The house overflowed out on the patio. All our friends from town were there, half the missions in the area were represented and we had one whale of an evening. Tears and laughter – ah yes, it was a grand affair!

Conclusion

Joyce is now living in Kongwa with Mary and little Betty, whom she had after leaving the ranch. Her people live near there, and with their help, her pombi trade and her maize shamba, she is managing. I hear from her periodically, taking her letters which are written in Swahili to an Asian girl to translate into English for me.

Helge and Liv now live in Pennsylvania where Helge has his own engineering firm. They now have another daughter, a sister for Camille. They came to see us and attended the wedding of one of our daughters.

Joseph Sipemba, the young doctor from Kilingala, is now in charge of that mission, as the Swedish doctor and his family left for home the year we returned to Canada.

Beth finished her schooling on returning to Canada and is married to Mitch Price. They have two little girls, Cheyenne and Chelsea, and live fifteen miles from our home.

I still feel that life is a learning experience and everything that happens, small and large, can be lesson material. What did I learn in my two years in Tanzania?

Probably the most important thing was the realization of how very little I did learn about the people and the country! I had always felt, since I was a small child, that God created human beings equal – all colors and creeds. My two years there just reinforced these thoughts.

I learned quickly that material things are not too important. I learned to appreciate the real things of value – everything else was so hard to get!

Would I go again? In a minute. So would Bill and Beth. We'd all love to go back and retrace our steps and visit everyone. There are still nights when I dream of Africa, of Joyce and the kids. Anyone who has ever spent any time in Africa can tell you – this vast, brooding continent gets in your blood and you're never quite the same again.

An unknown author penned these lines which best describe

119

my feelings about my African experience:

"Moths will scorch their wings
but soon will return
Their love of light
Is greater than their sense
of pain."